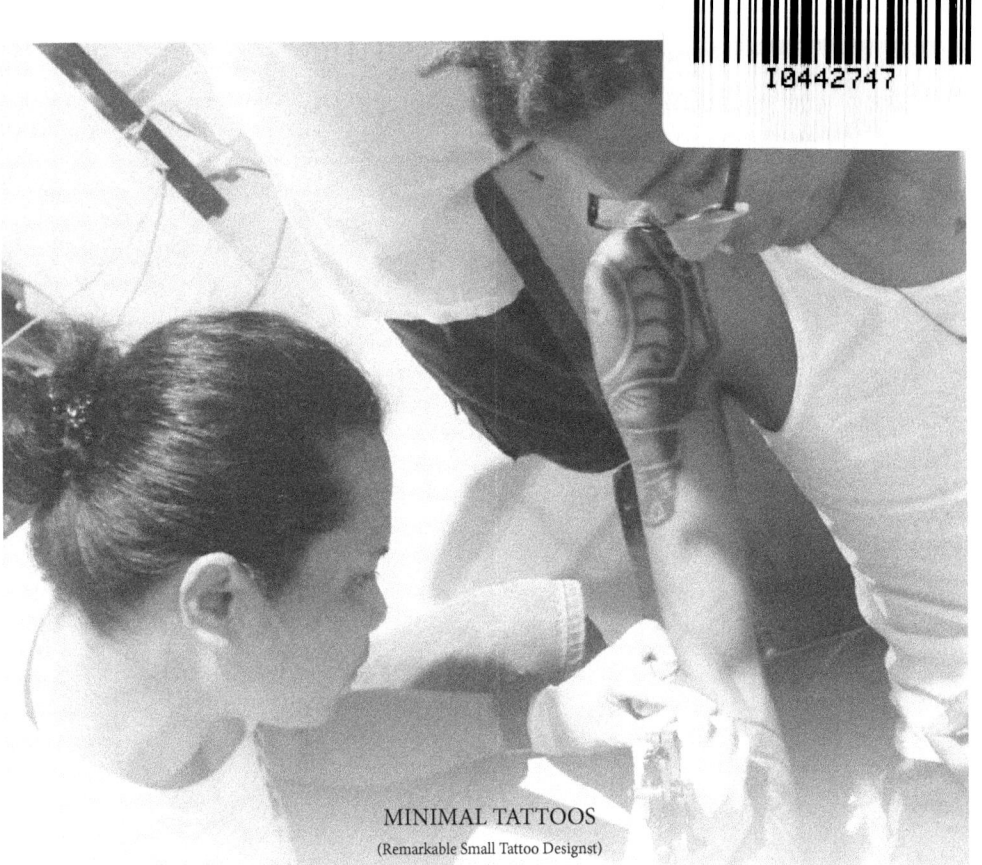

MINIMAL TATTOOS
(Remarkable Small Tattoo Designst)

This is the NEW and ADVANCED modern book of trending and meaningful minimal, small or flash tattoo design symbols in the tattoo world. A perfect reference book for Tattoo beginners or even for Professional Tattoo Artists. All design content are drawn or illustrated and categorized properly so that you will effortlessly find what type of design you are looking for during your tattoo session, study or practice.

Here are some list of the remarkable designs:

Geometric Designs

Traditional design

Symbols / Magical / Runes / Zodiac Signs

Animals / Eagles / Reptiles / Bear / Tiger / Birds

Bodies / Eyes / Hands / Pinup

Landscape / Waves / Plants / Flowers / Leaves

Cool Stuffs / Shoes / Cigarette / Cards / Games / Foods

Musical / Instruments / Notes

Skulls / Butterflies / Stones

Arrows / Ornamental

All rights reserved.

No part of this book may be reproduced, distributed or transmitted in any form or by any means, including recording, photocopying, or other electronic methods, without the prior written permission of the publisher.

ISBN: 979-8-5852-50736

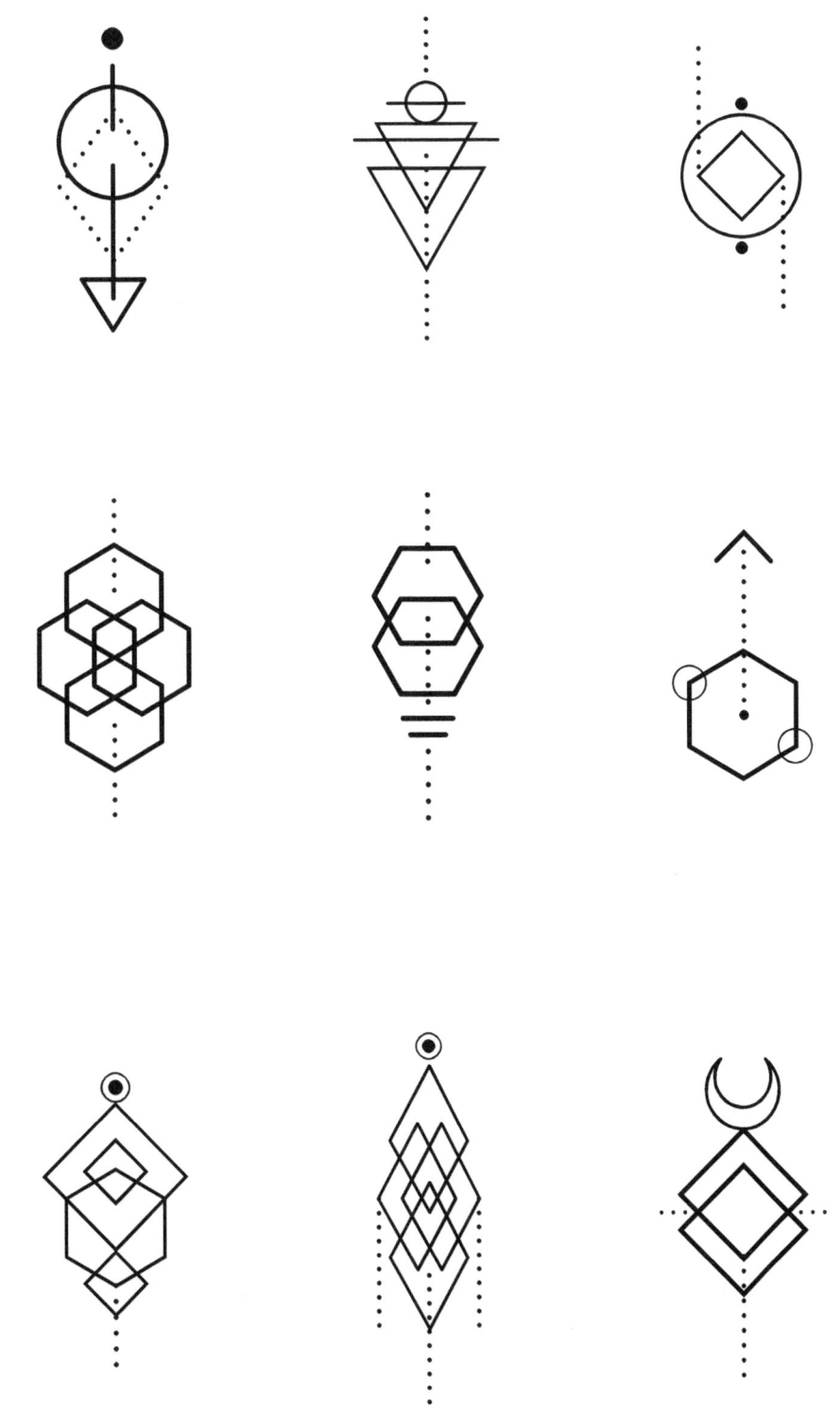

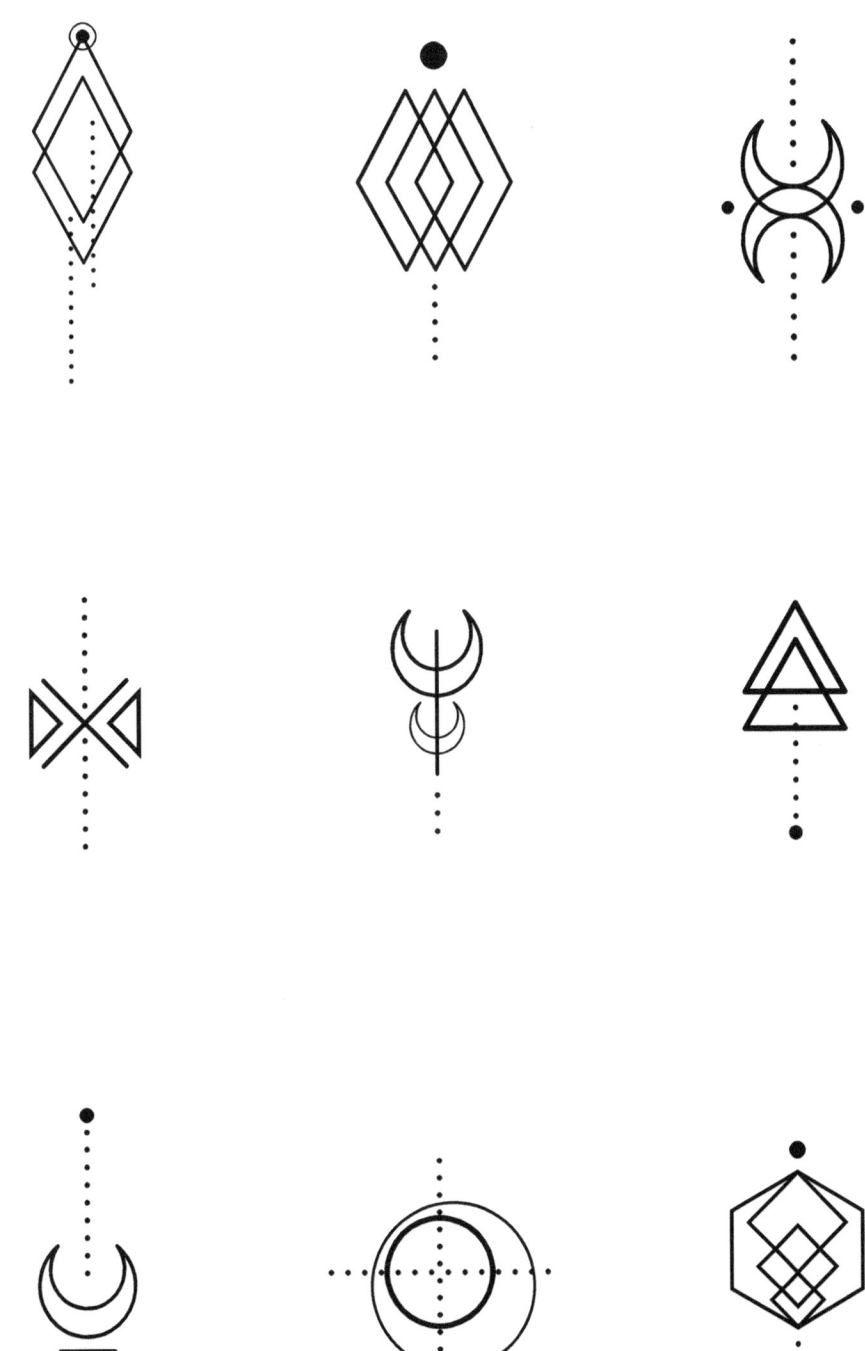

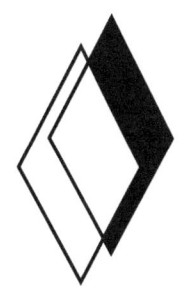
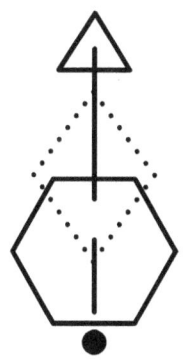
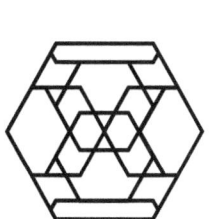
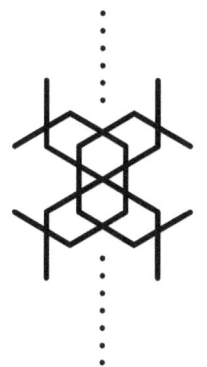
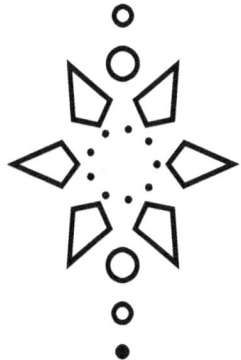
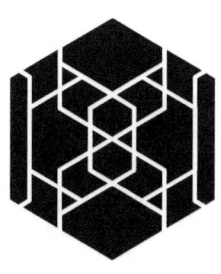

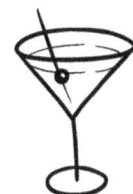 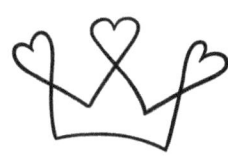 
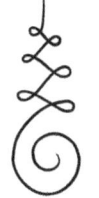 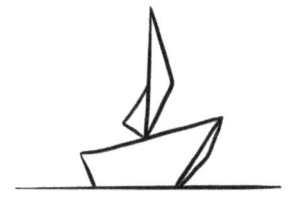 
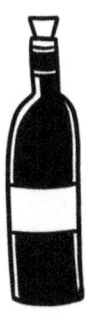 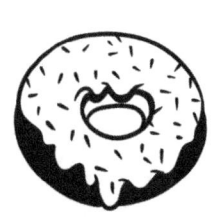 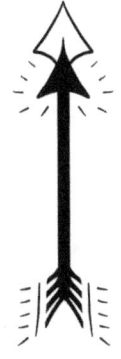

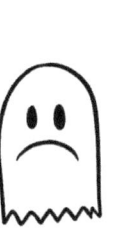

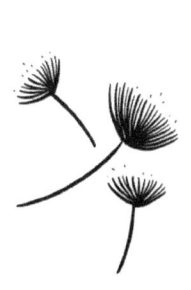

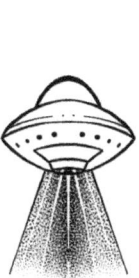
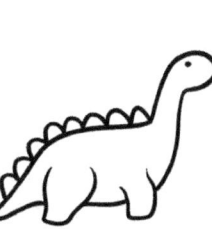

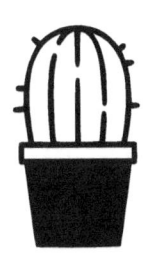 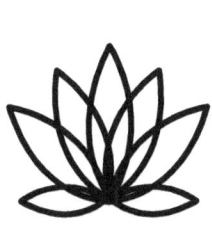 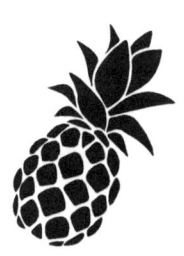
 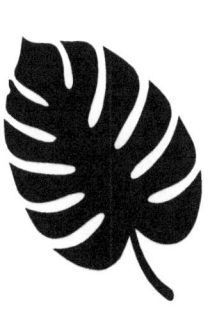 
 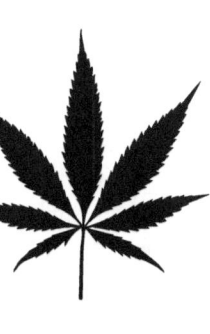 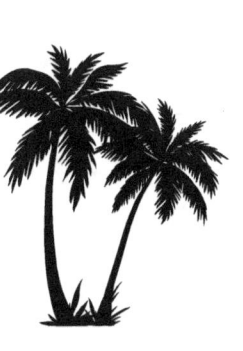
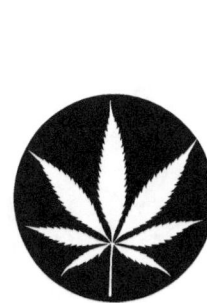  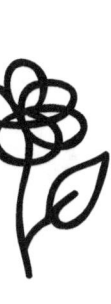

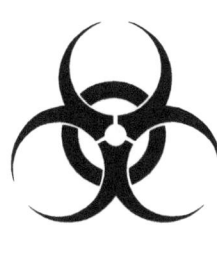 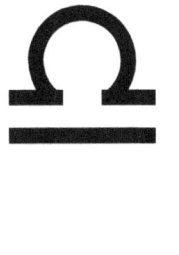 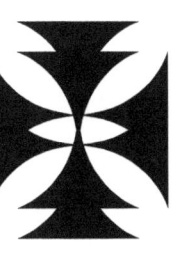

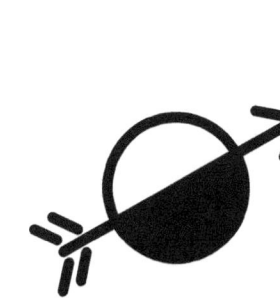 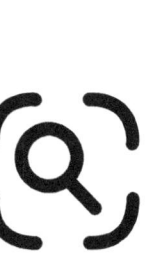 

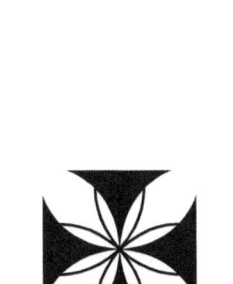 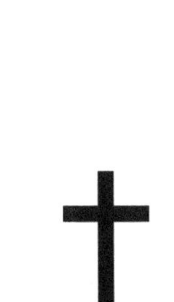 

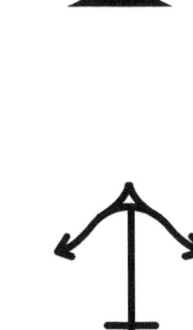  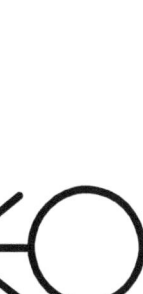

 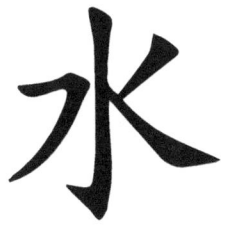 

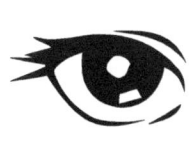 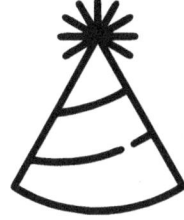 

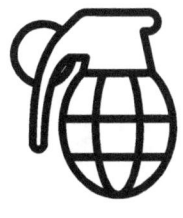 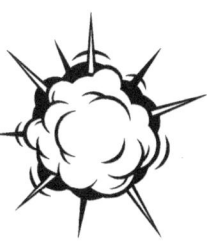 

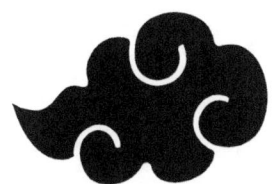 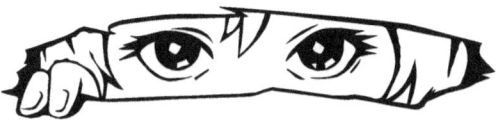

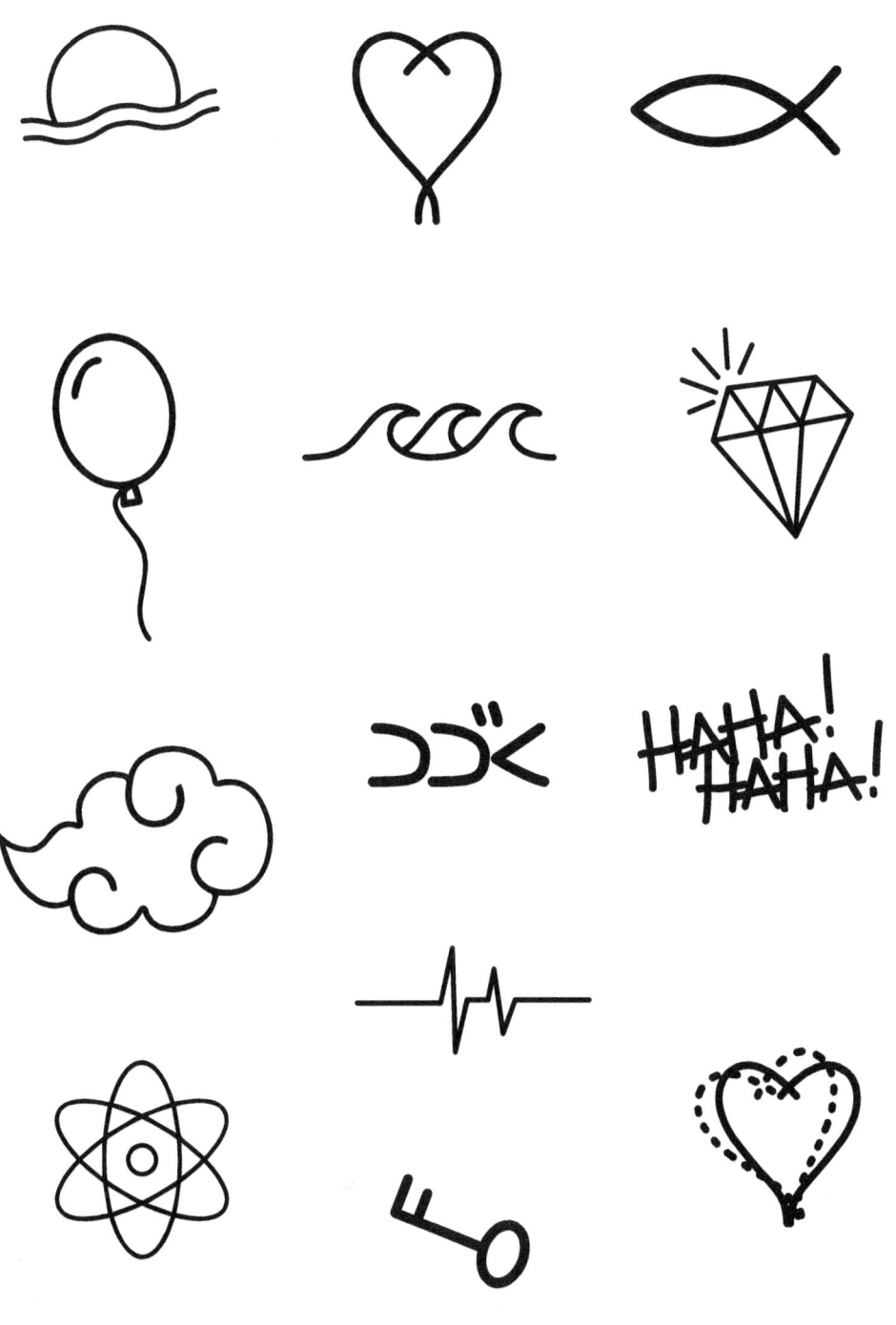

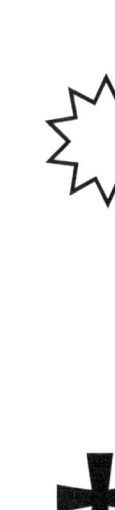

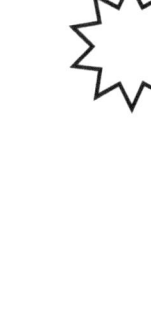

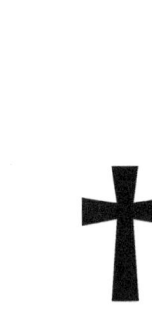
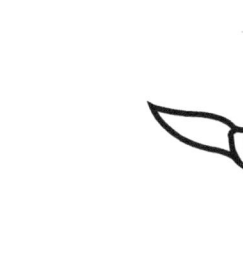

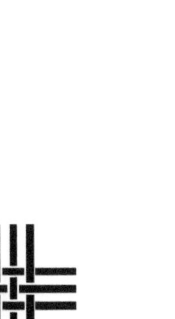

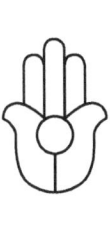

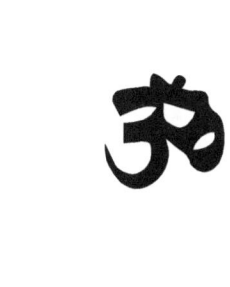

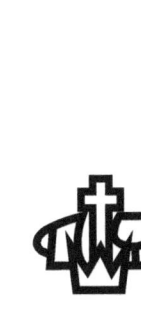

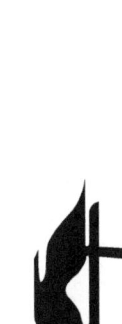
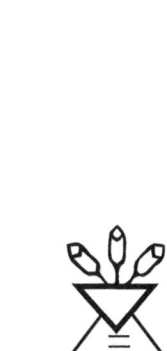

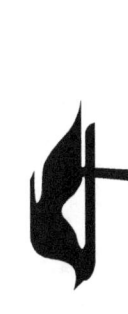
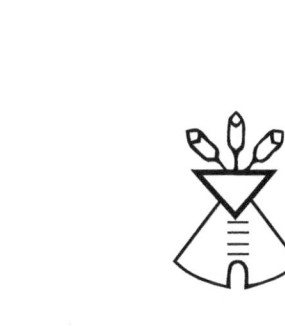

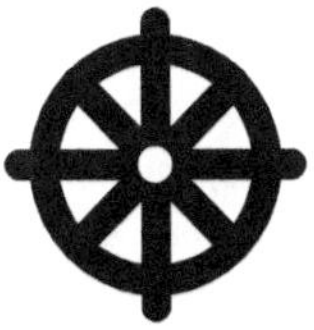

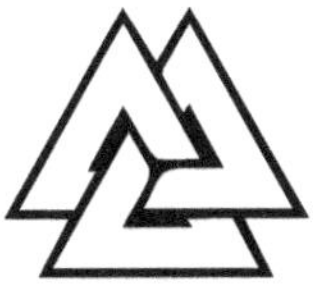

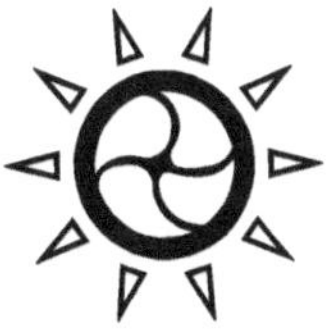

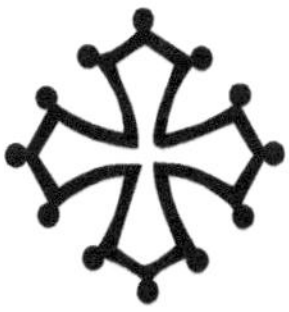

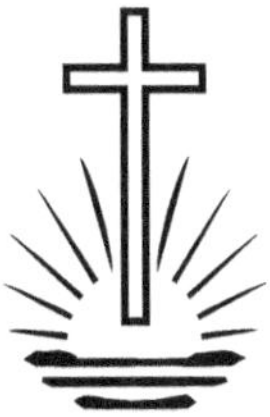

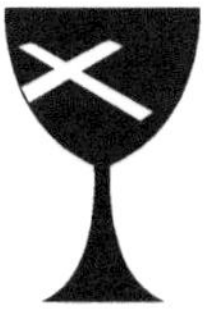

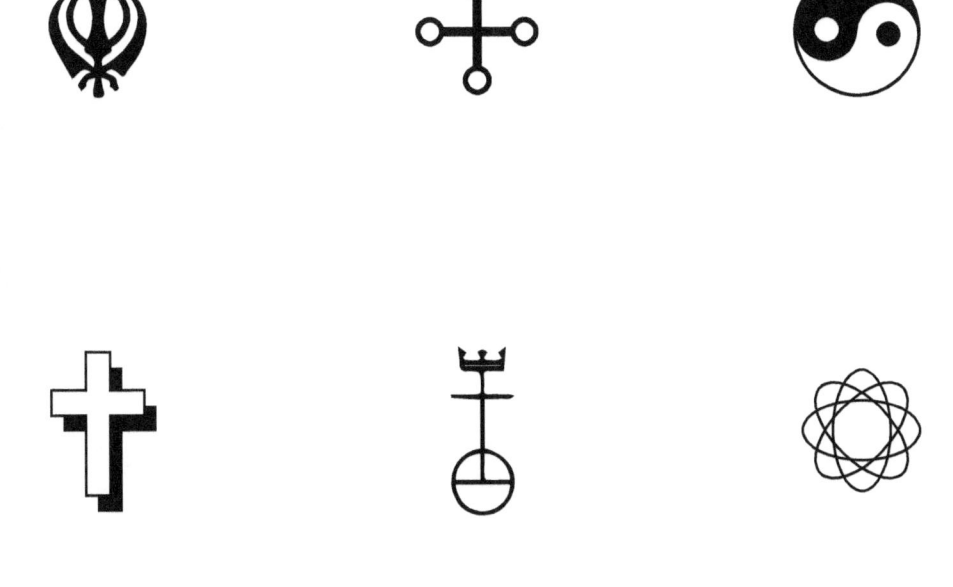

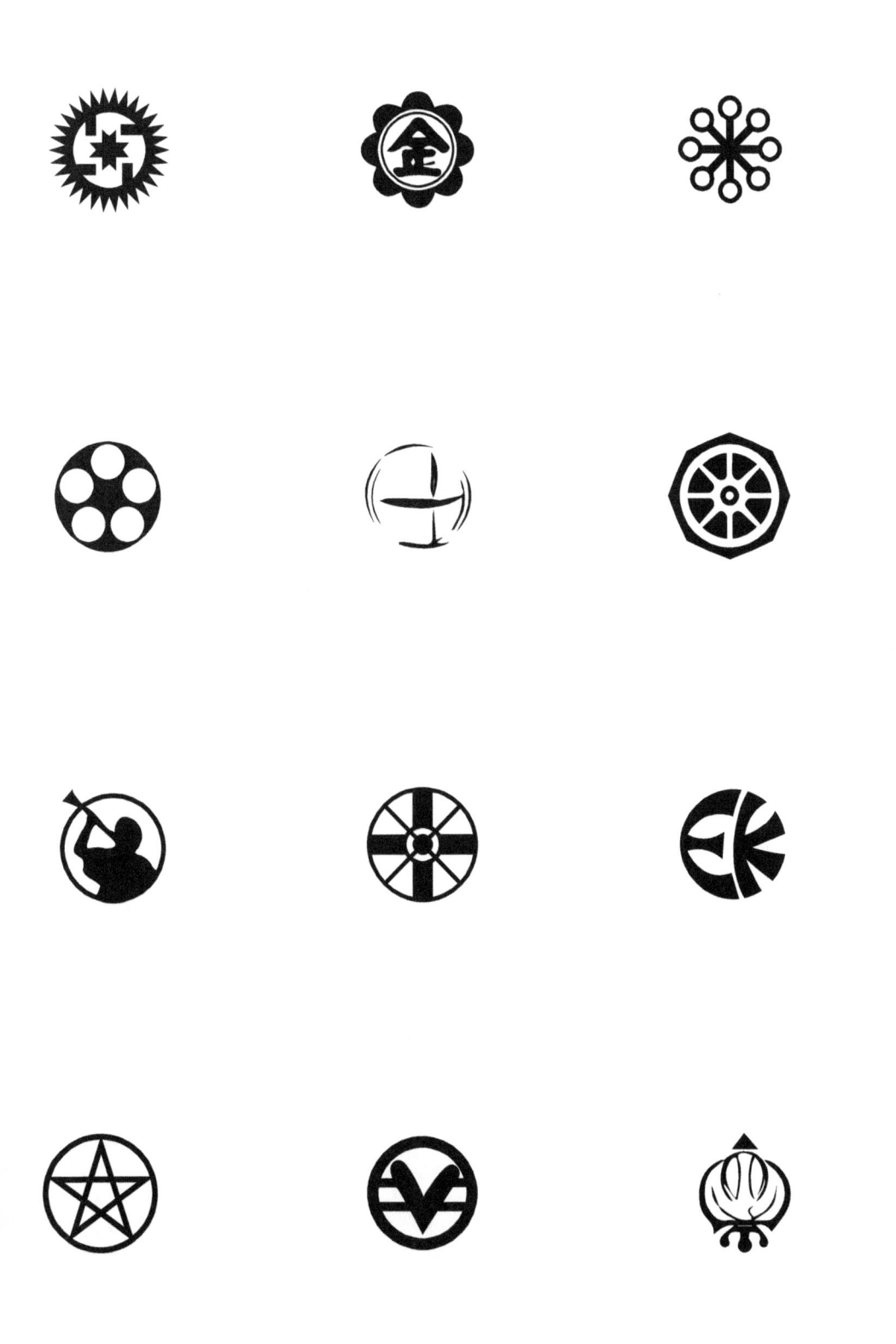

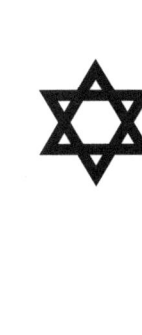
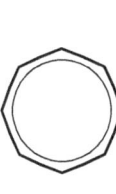
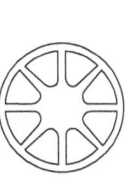
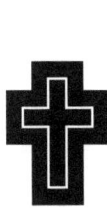
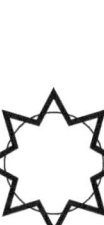
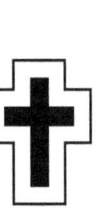
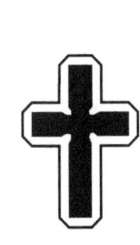
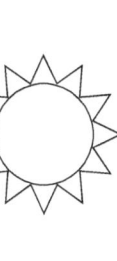
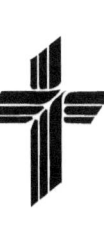
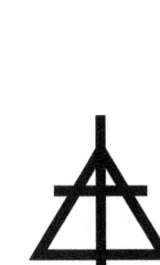

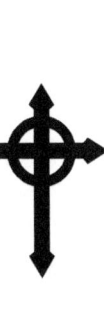

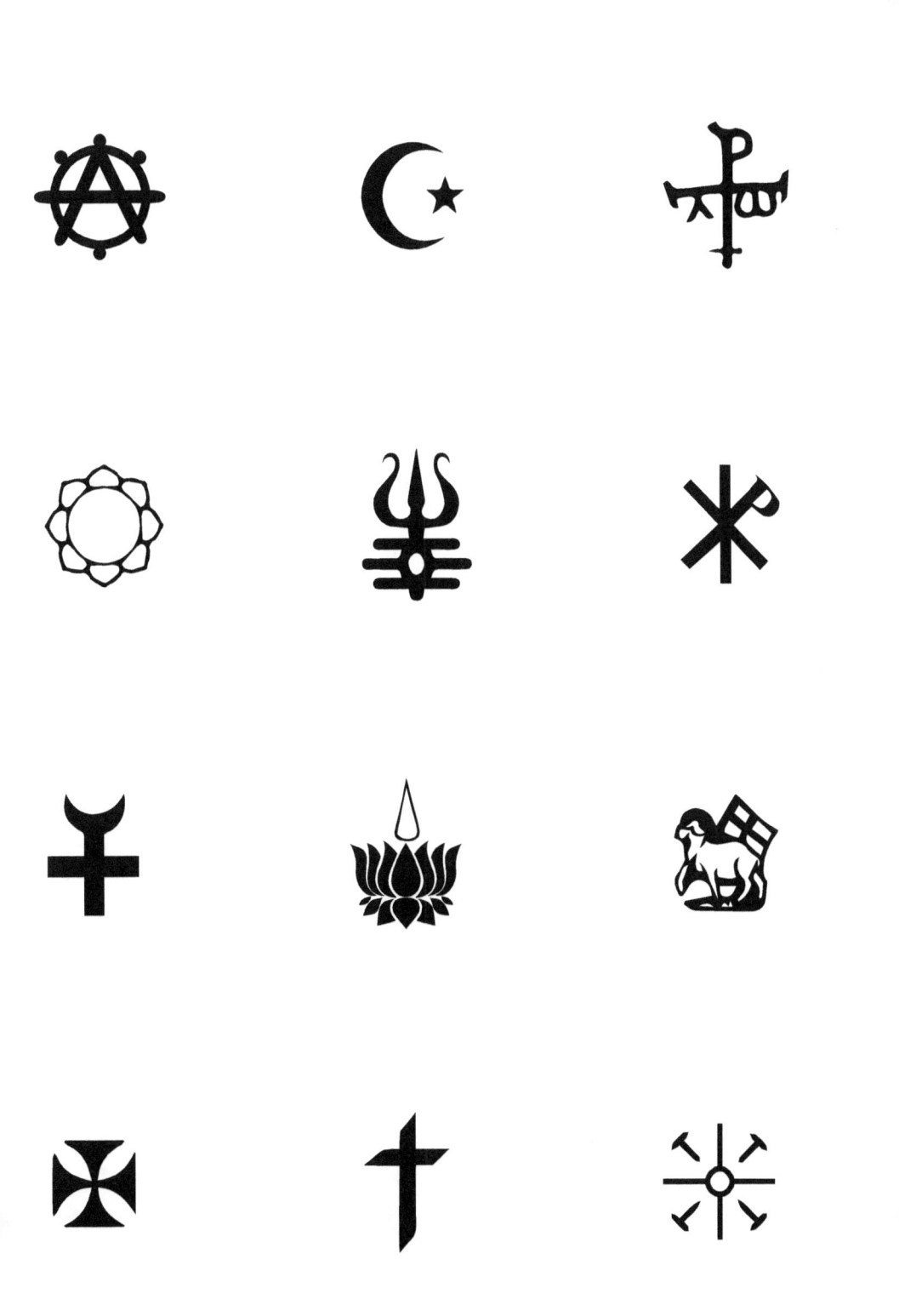

Angelic Zibu Symbols

Abu: Sacred Unity

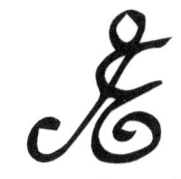
Akunate: Centeredness

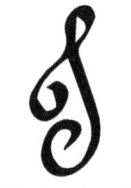
Ani: Nurture Yourself

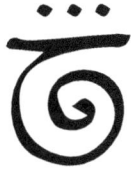
Atu: Persistence

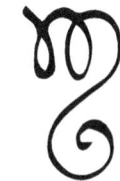
Atuna: Release Expectations

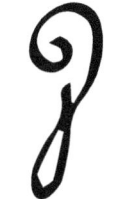
Anoko: Patience

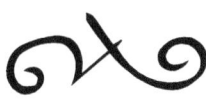
Anona: Fortitude

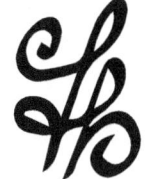
Anu: Gratitude

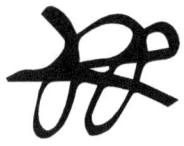
Arani: Beauty

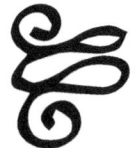
Asi: Authenticity

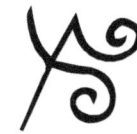
Awanda: Encouragement

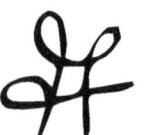
Habukana: Effortless Connection

Hamada: Vitality

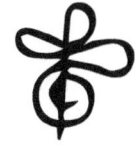
Hana: Peacekeeper

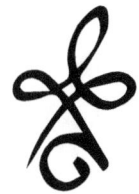
Hatumi: Acceptance of Optimum Health

 Hazu: Kindness
 Huka: Awakening
 Imono: Creativity
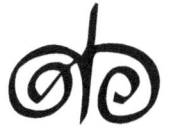 Imu: Divine Essense

 Kalu: SynthesisK
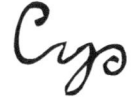 unata: Nature
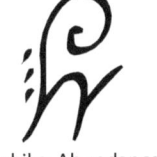 Lahika: AbundanceM
 atanu: Receptivity

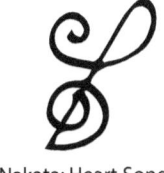 Nakata: Heart Song
 Rasini: Embrace Life
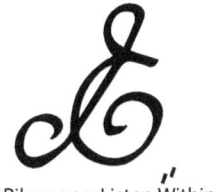 Rikumana: Listen Within
 Sati: Beacon of Hope

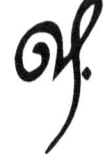 Shikawa: Sacred PlaceS
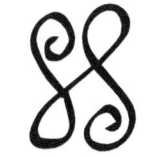 okana: TransitionT
 akama: ReciprocityT
 ama: Friendship

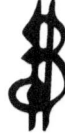 Tatama: Order out of Chaos
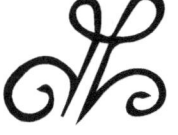 Tatina: Willingness
 Tina: Thrive Present Mpment
 Ziwa: Universal Love

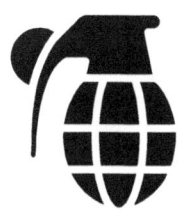
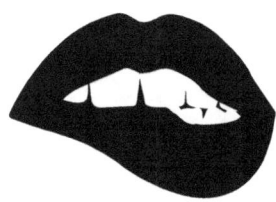
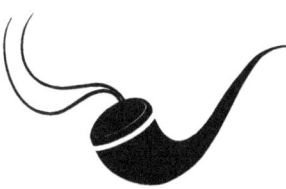
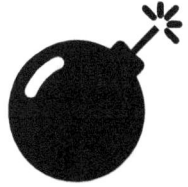
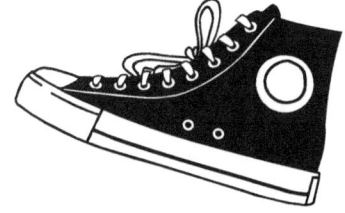
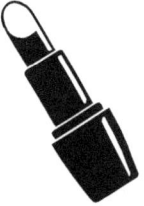
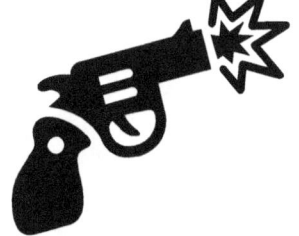

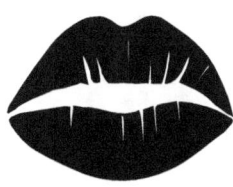
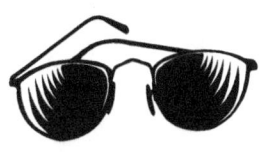
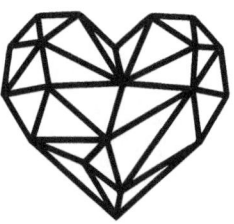
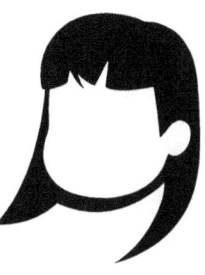

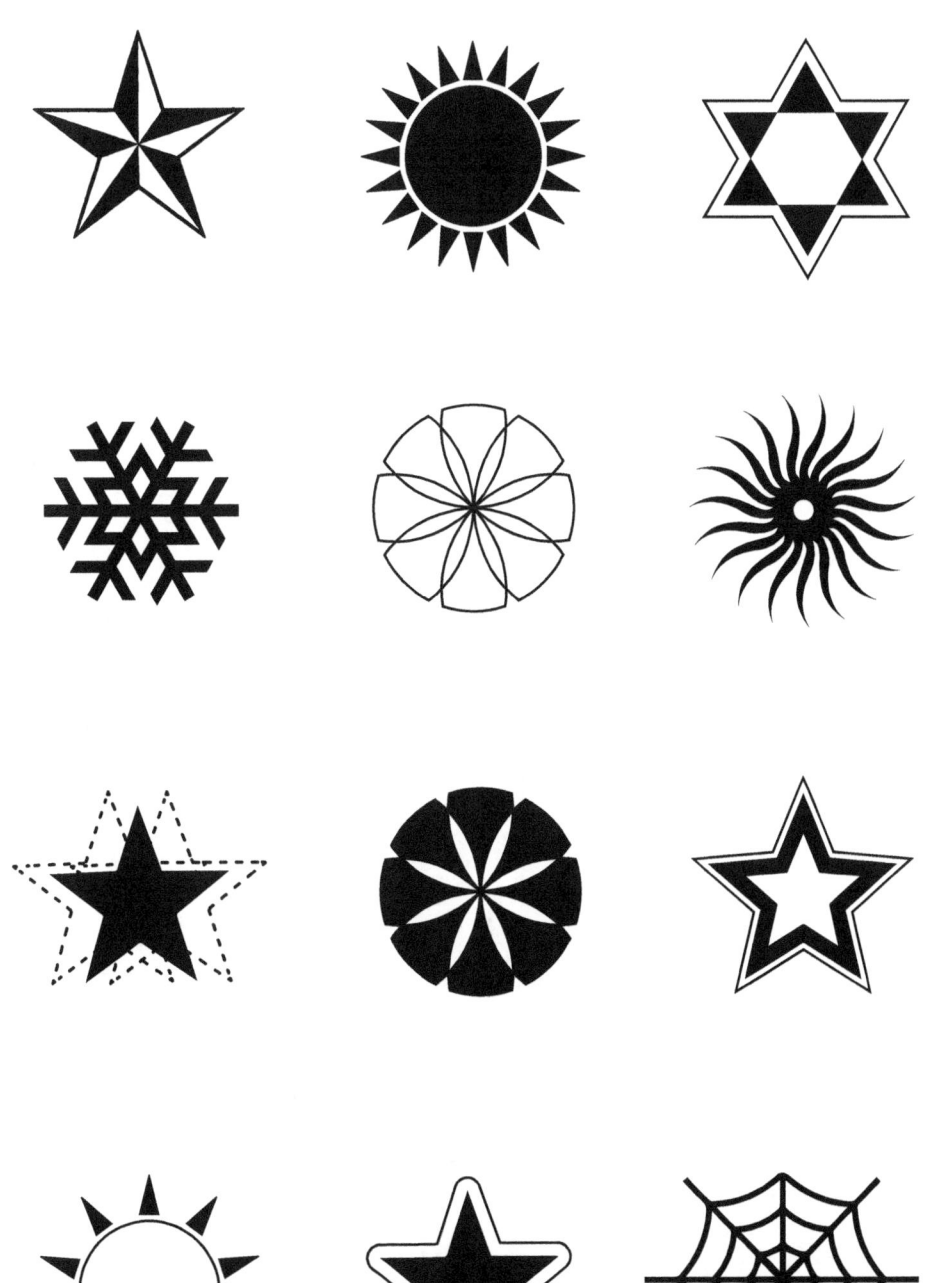

♏ ♈ ♌

♉ ♍ ♑

♐ ♒ ♎

♊ ♓ ♋

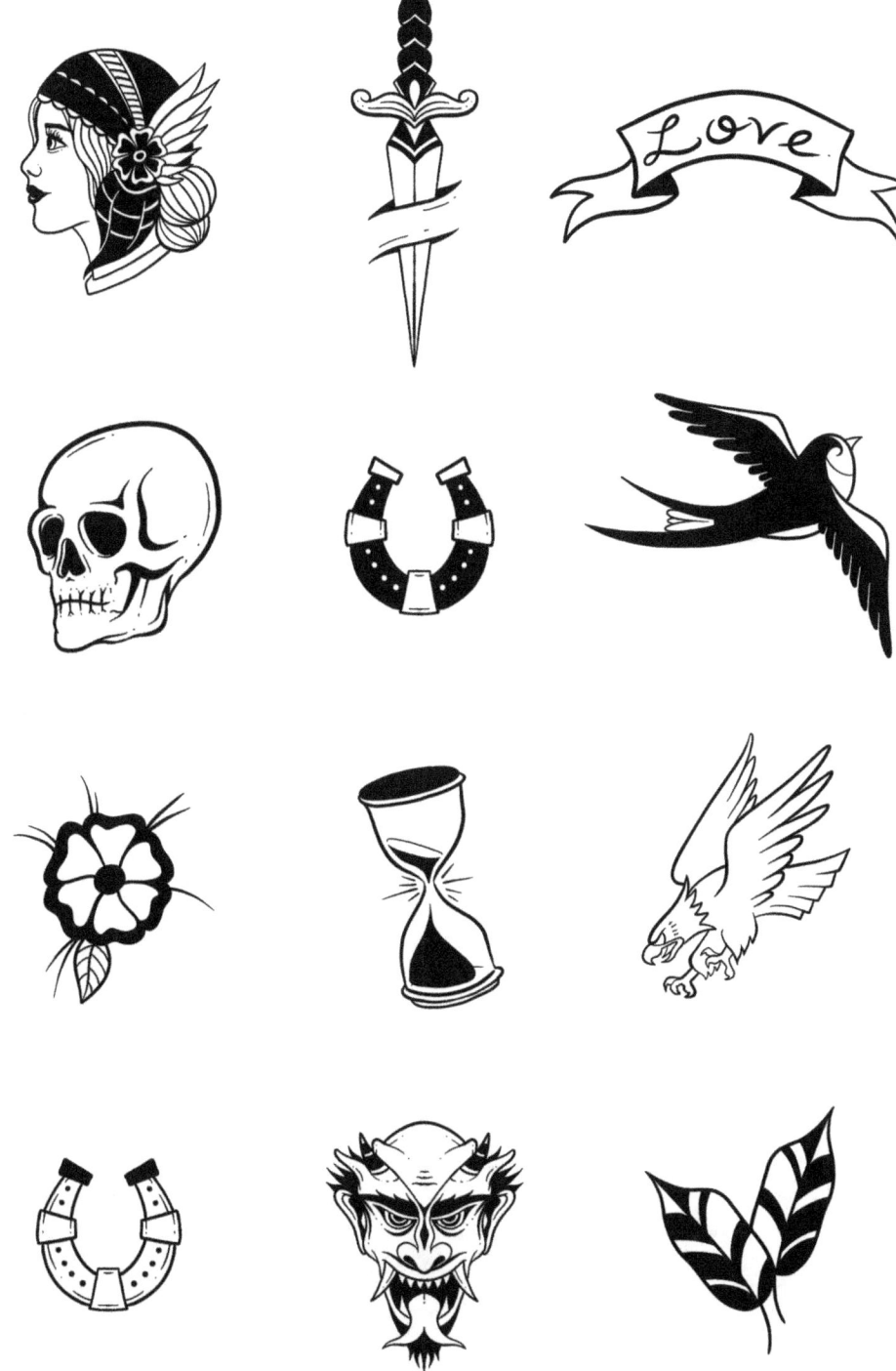

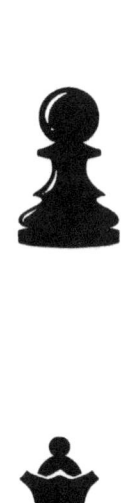
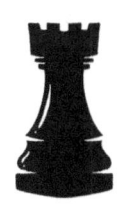
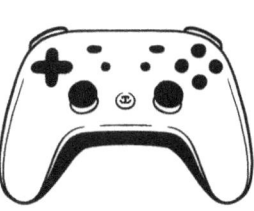
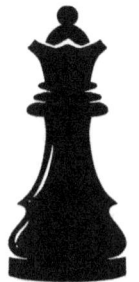
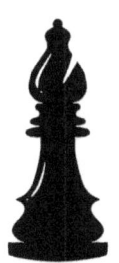
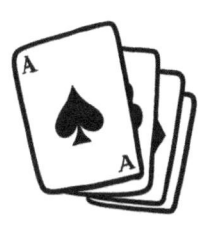
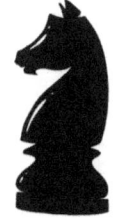
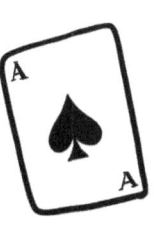
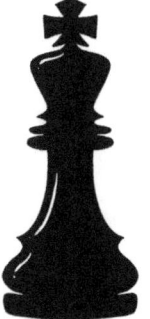
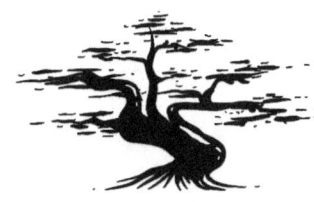
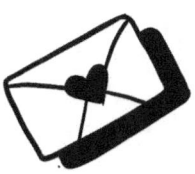
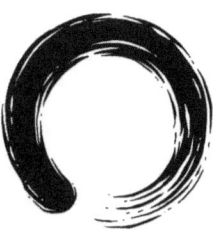

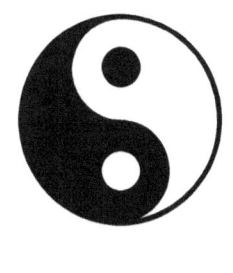  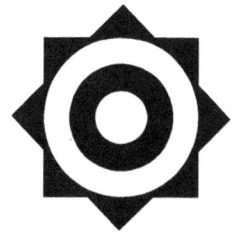

 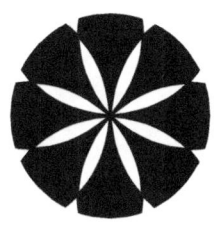 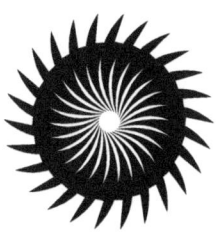
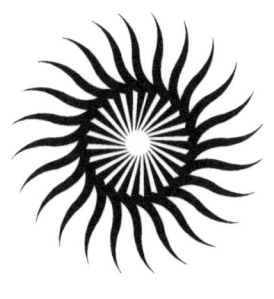 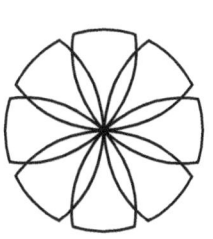 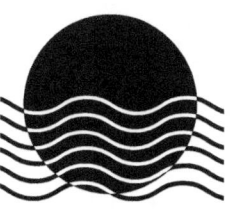

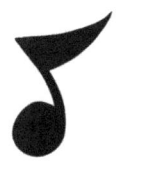 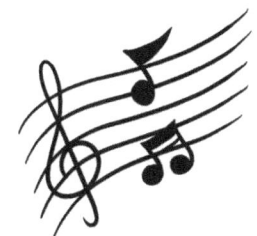 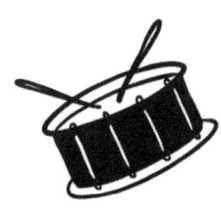
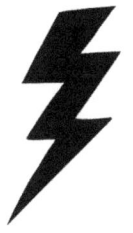  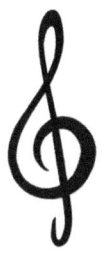
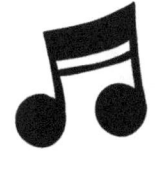 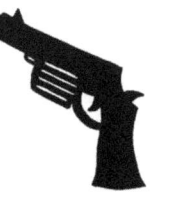 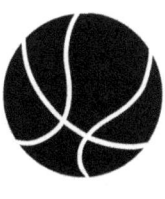
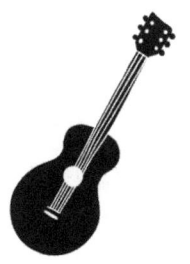 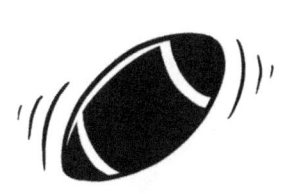 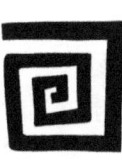

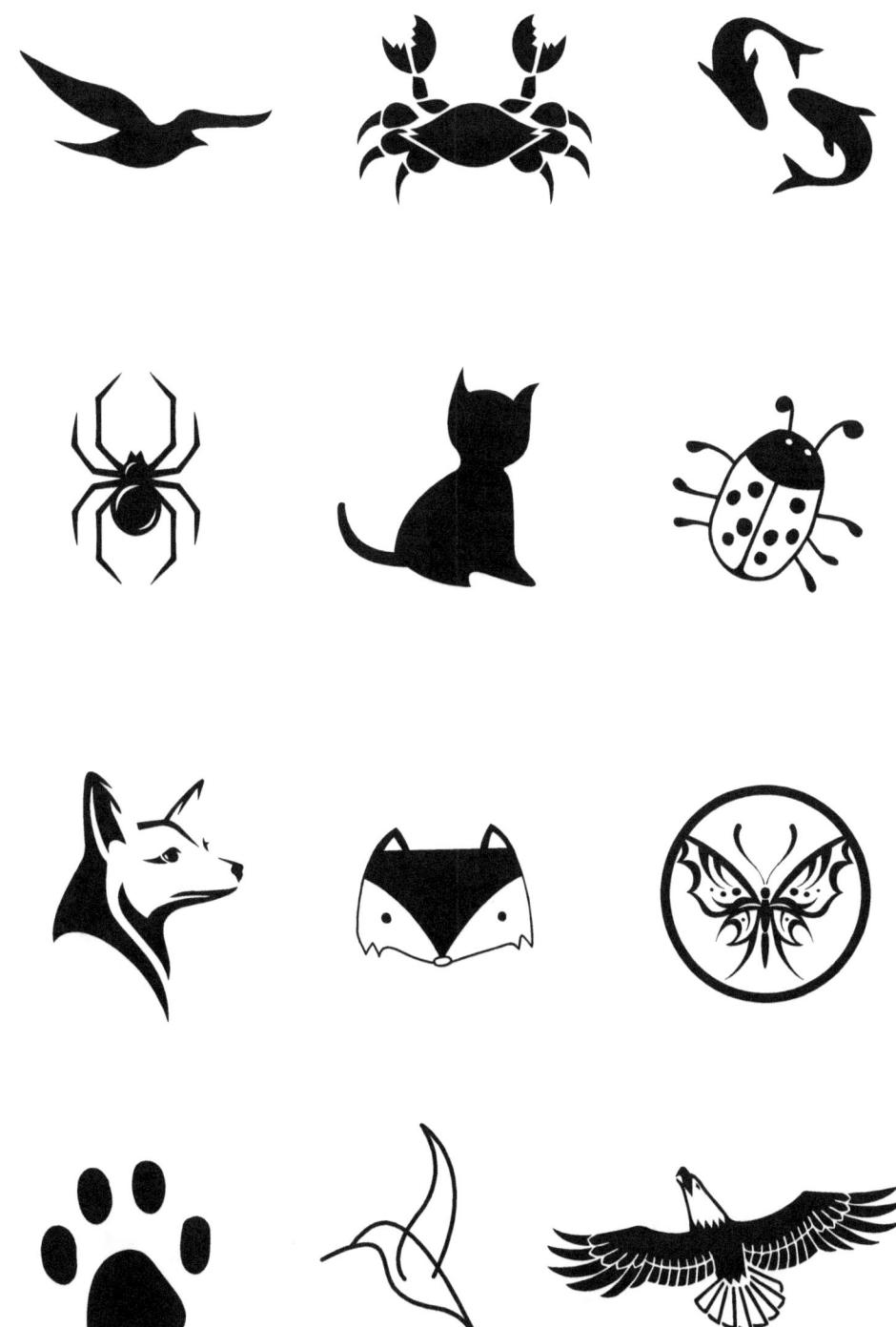

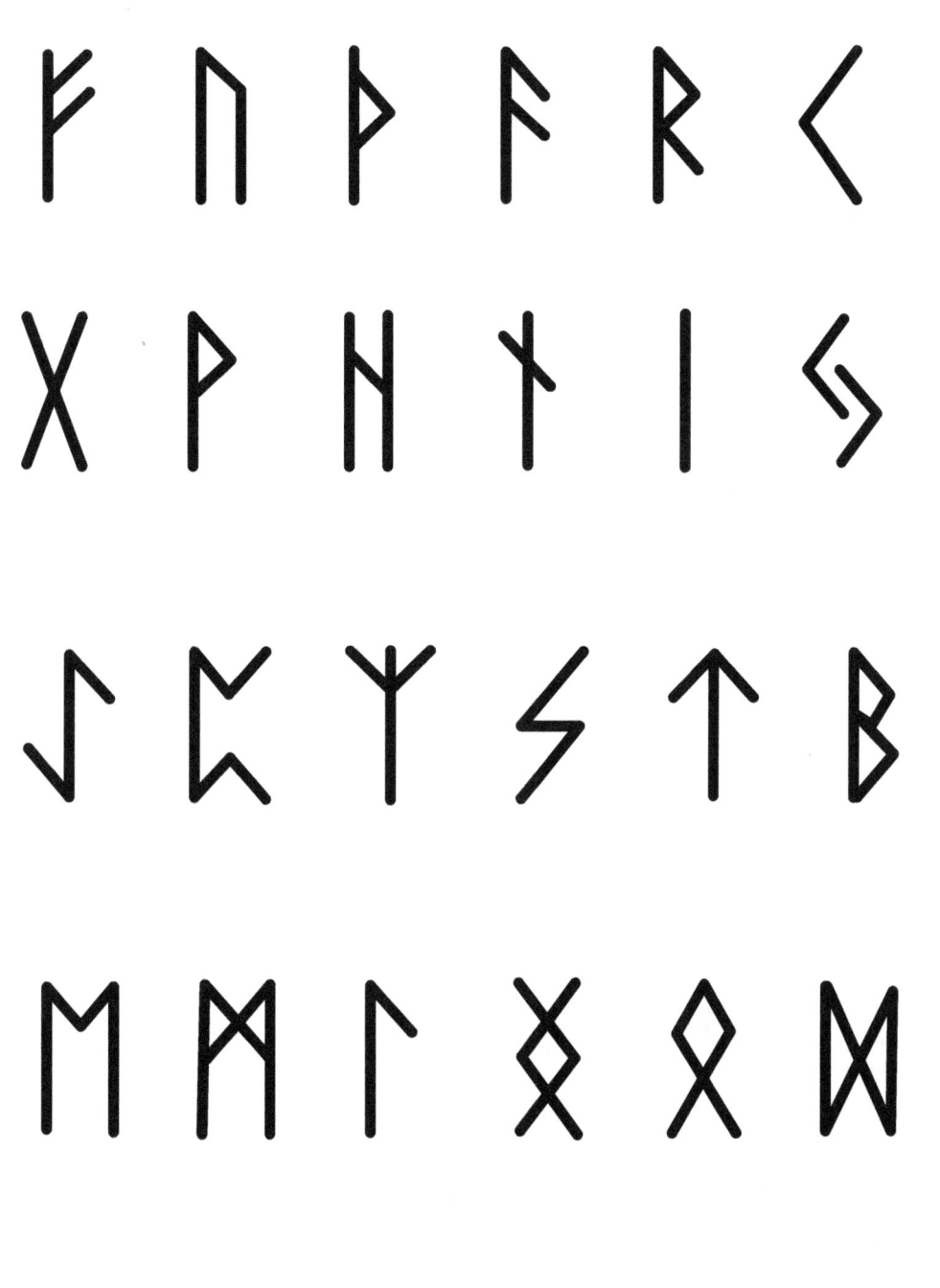

  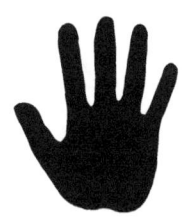
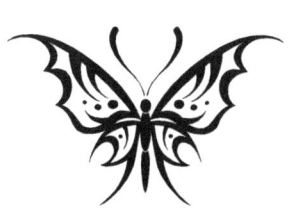 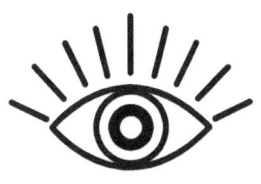 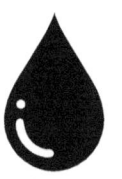
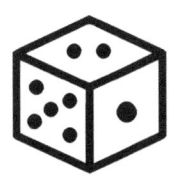 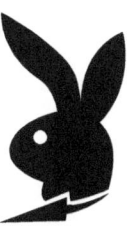 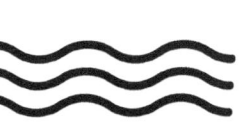
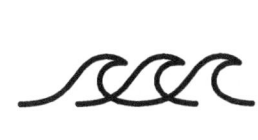 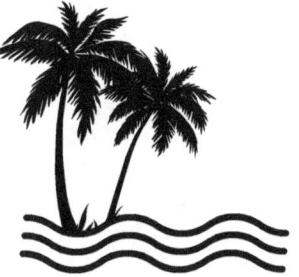 

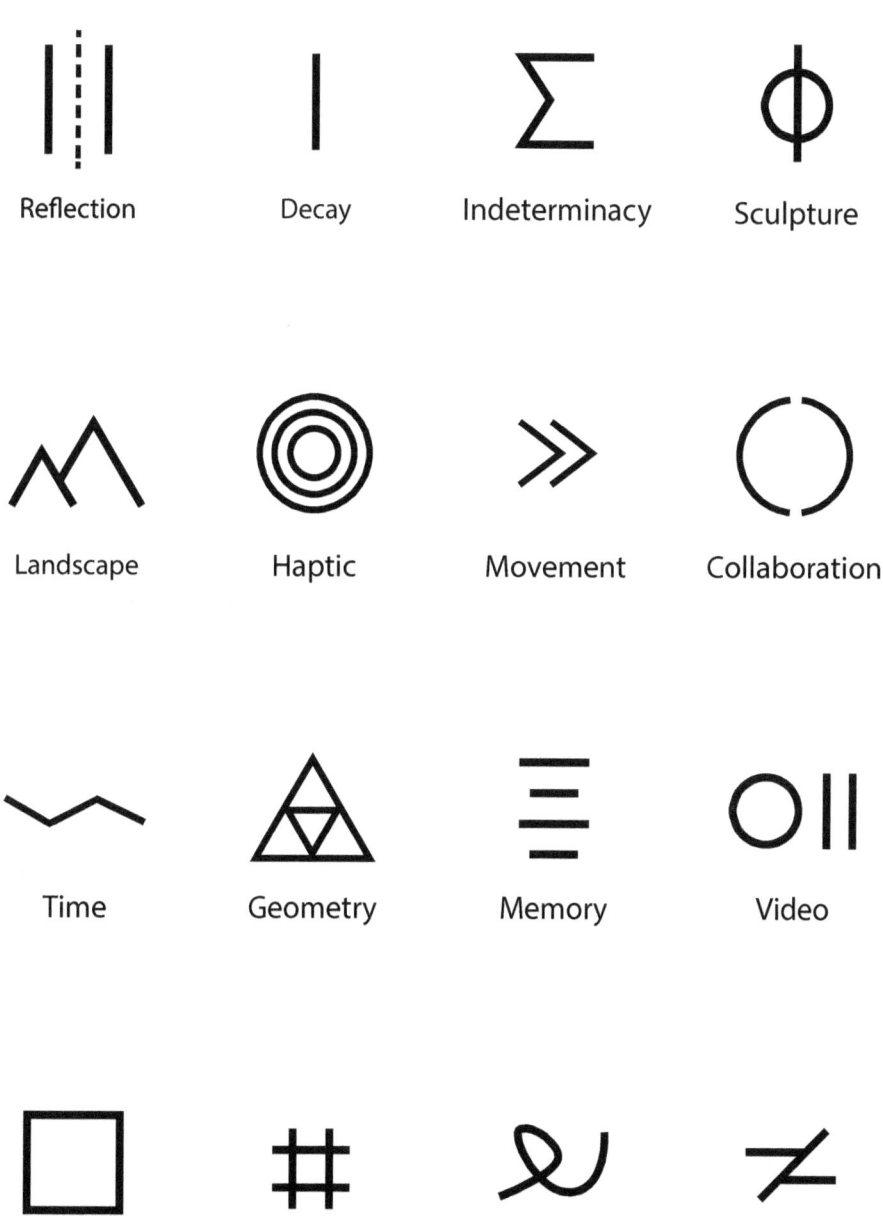

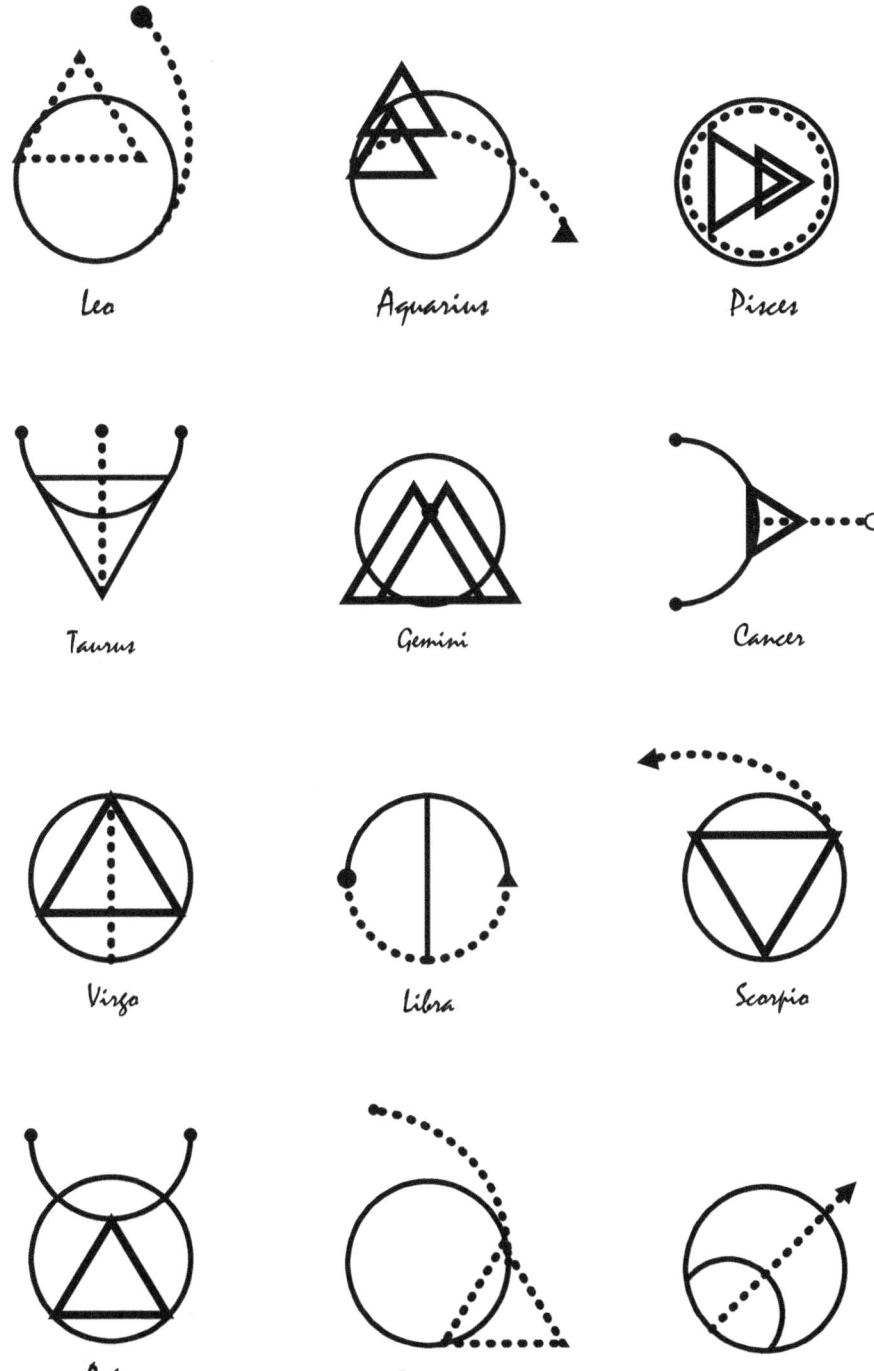

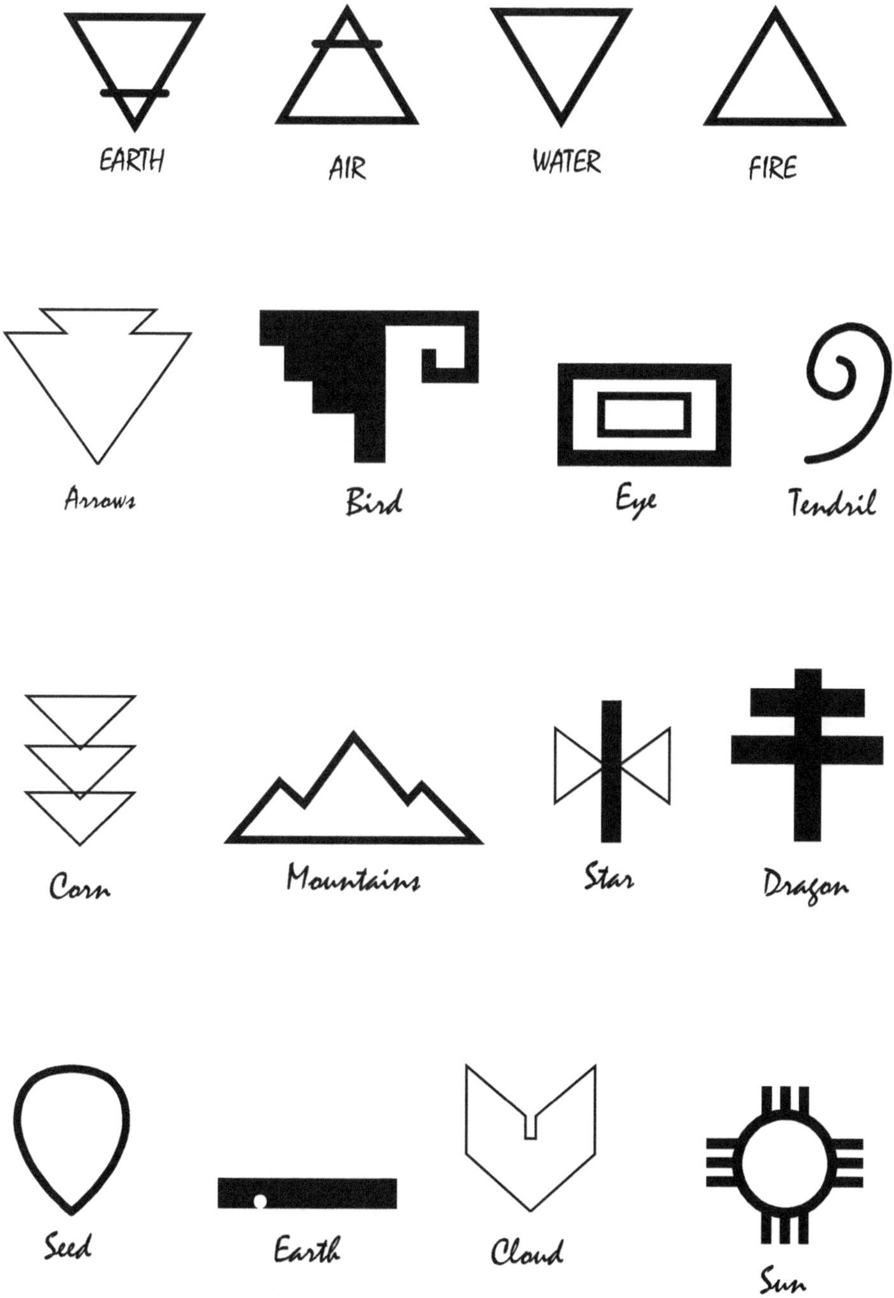

EARTH	AIR	WATER	FIRE
Arrows	Bird	Eye	Tendril
Corn	Mountains	Star	Dragon

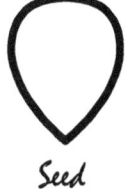
Seed

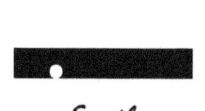
Earth

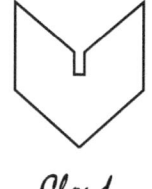
Cloud

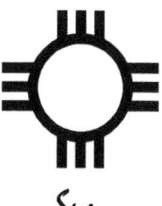
Sun

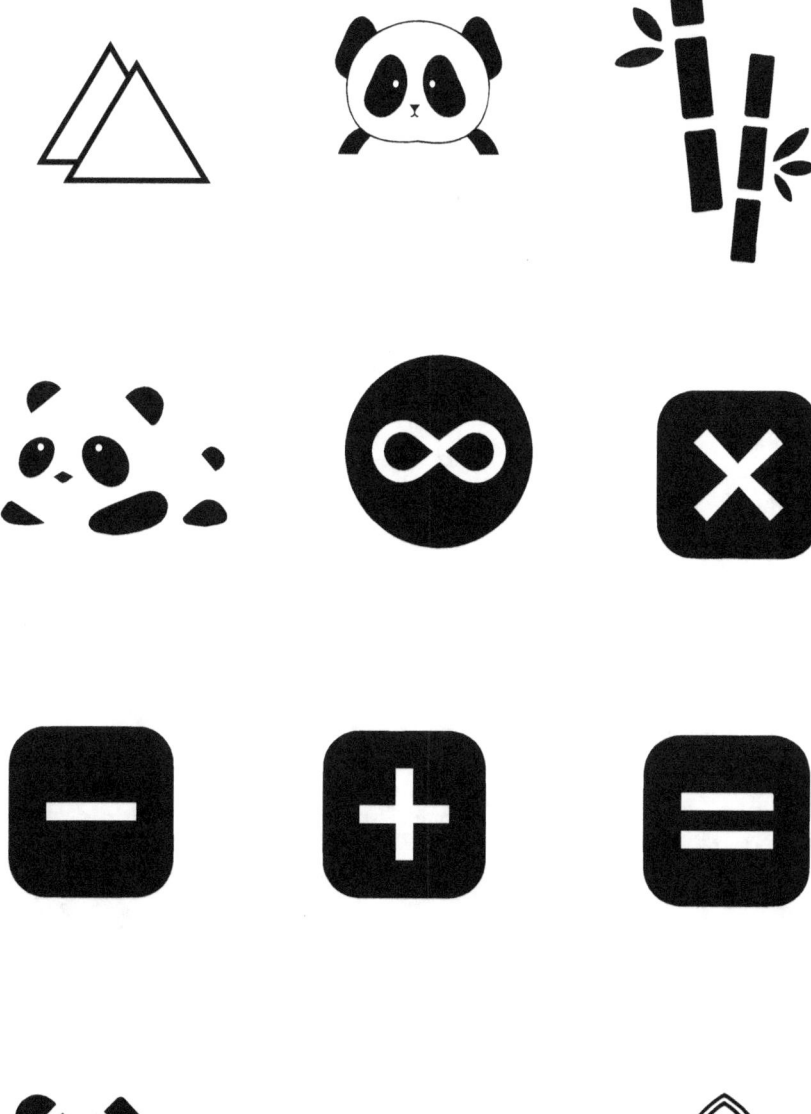

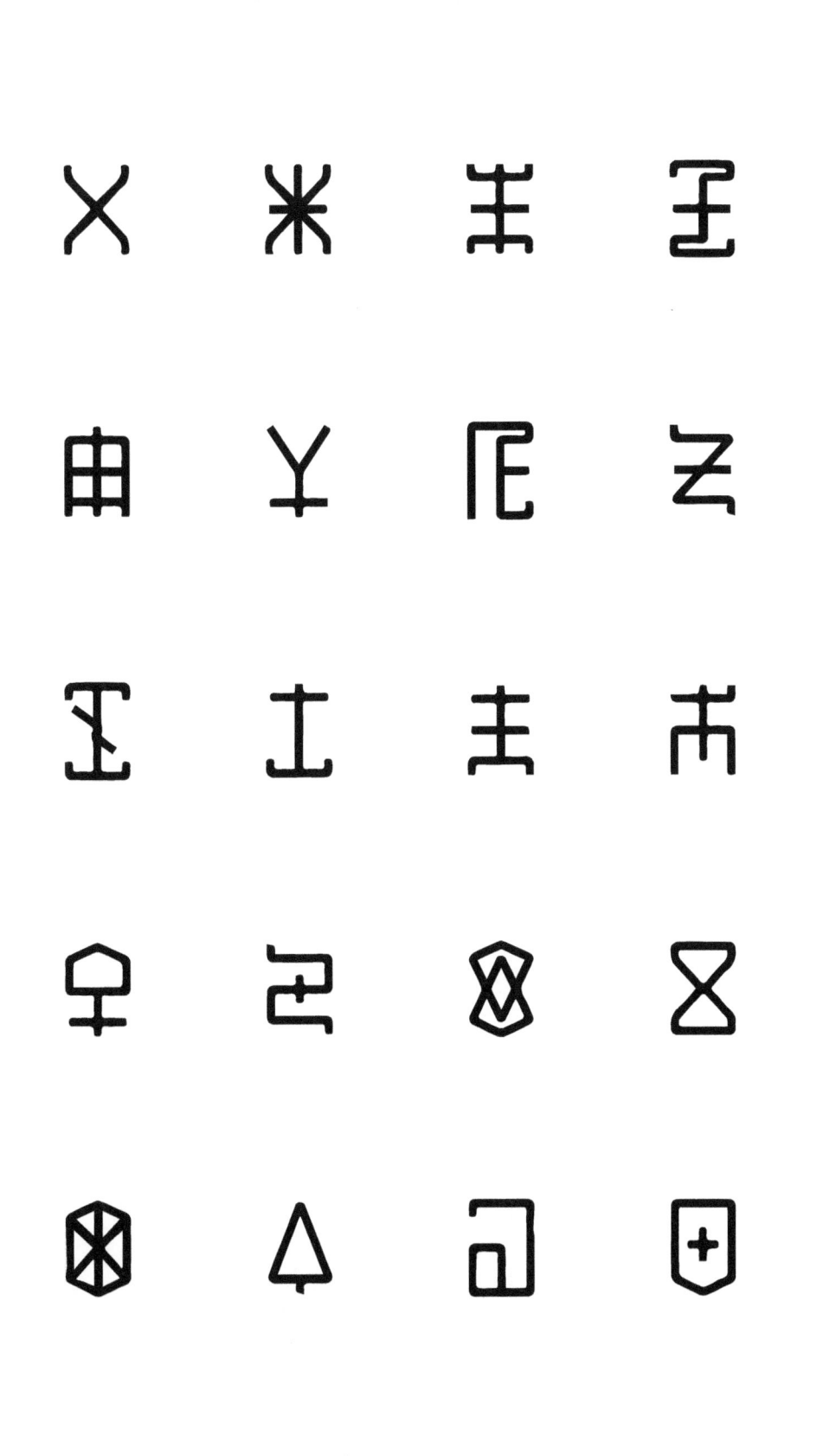

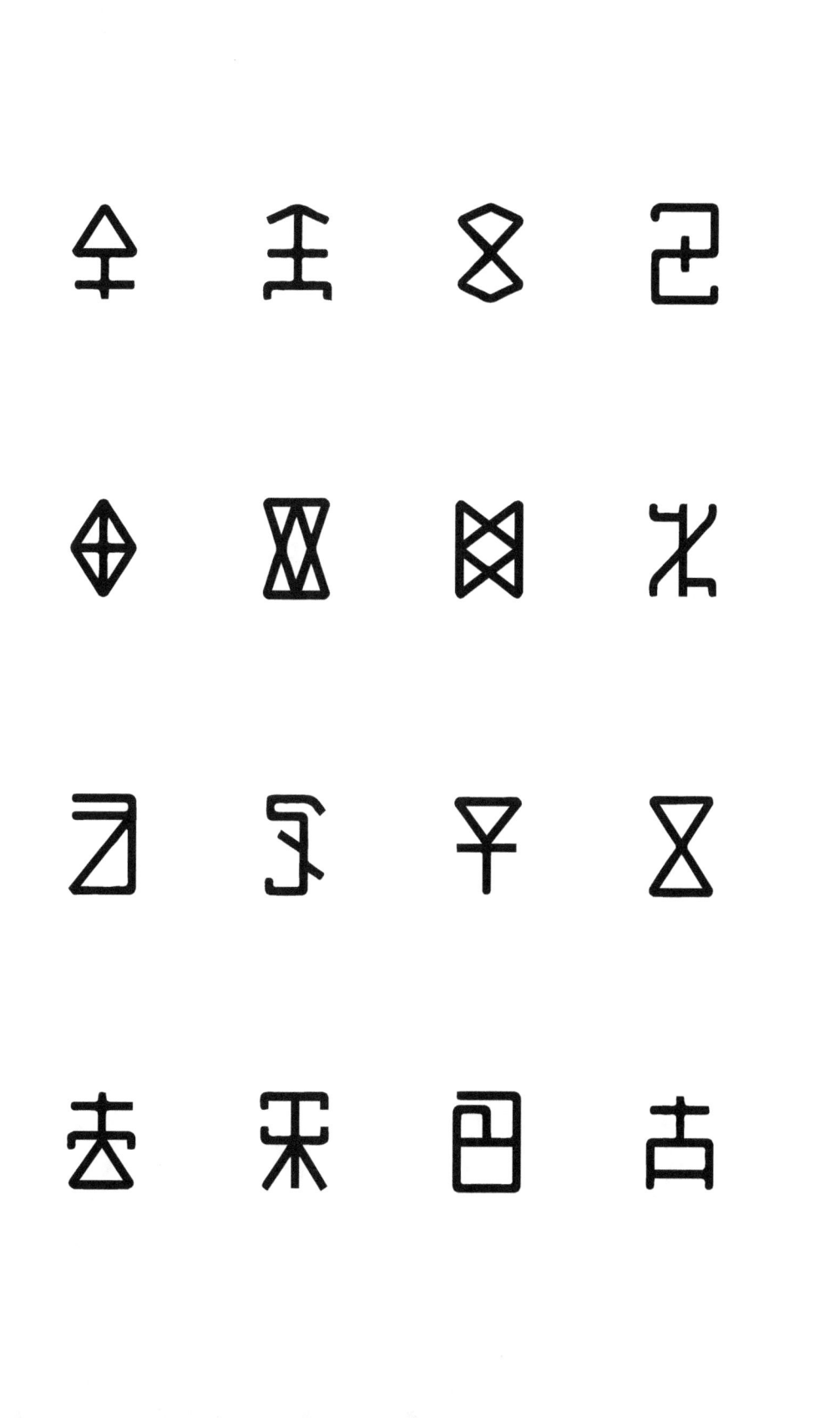

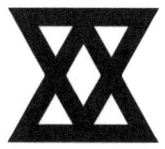
CONNECT

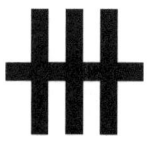
FRIENDS

UNDERSTAND

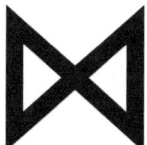
REFLECT

TRANSCEND

CHALLENGE

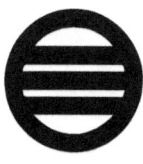
POWER

EXPRESS

COMBINE

HOME

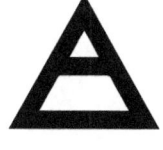
EXPLORE

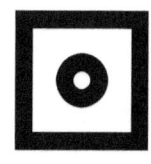
TRUTH

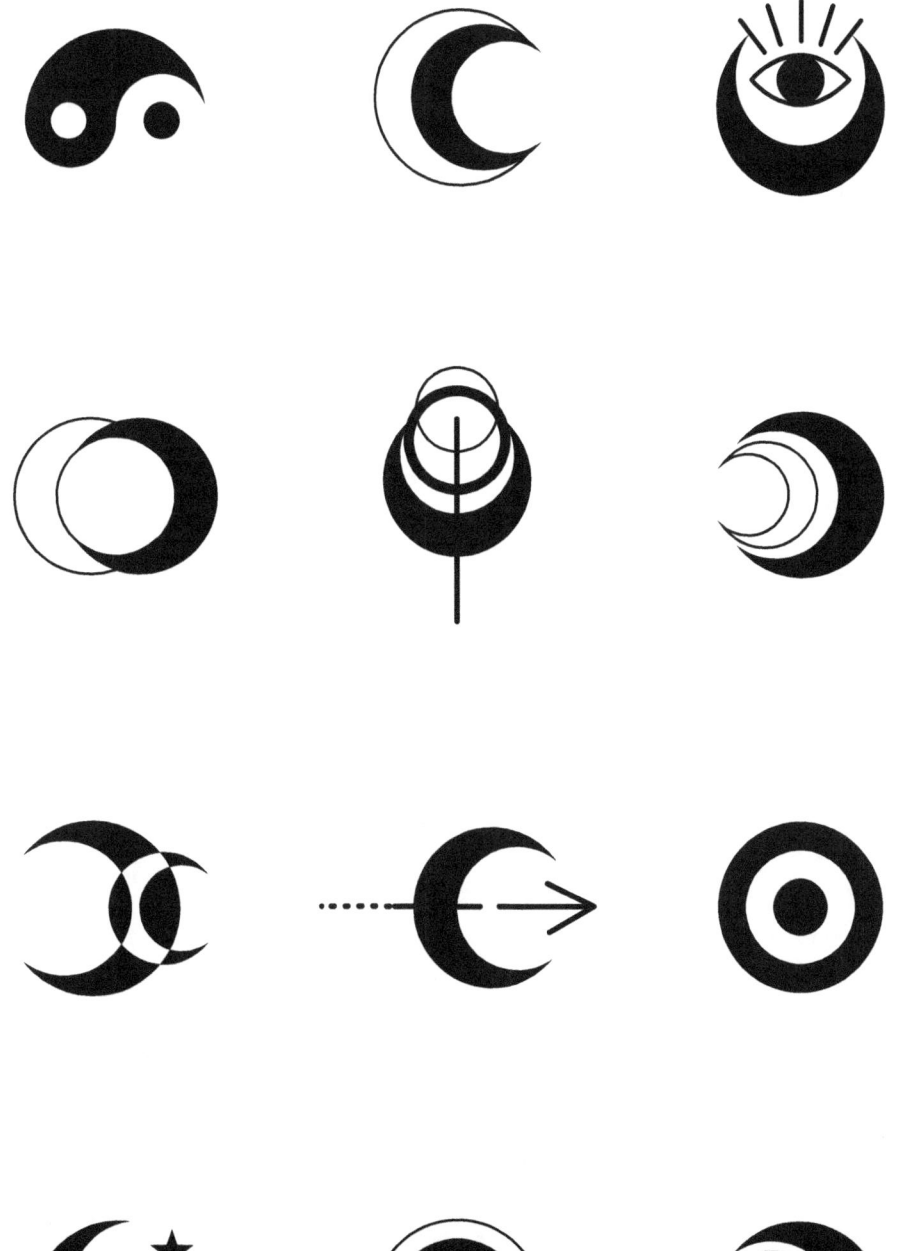

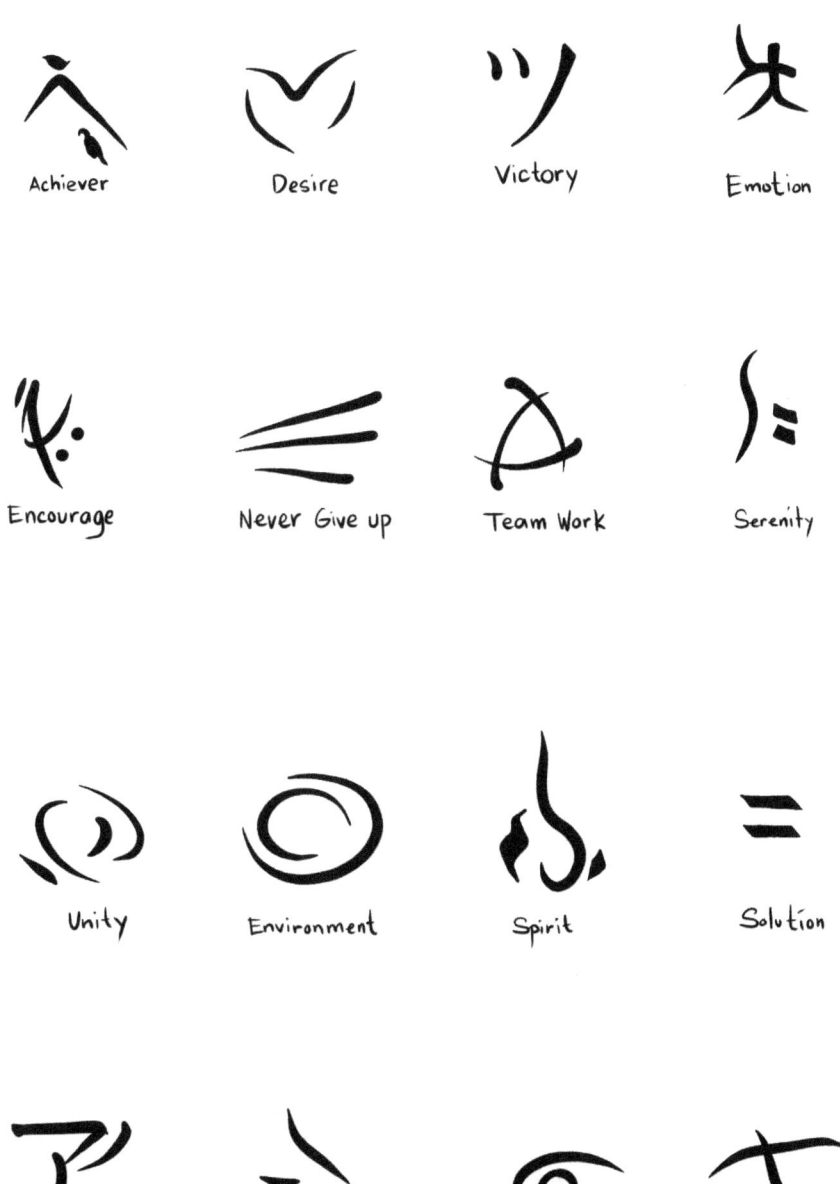

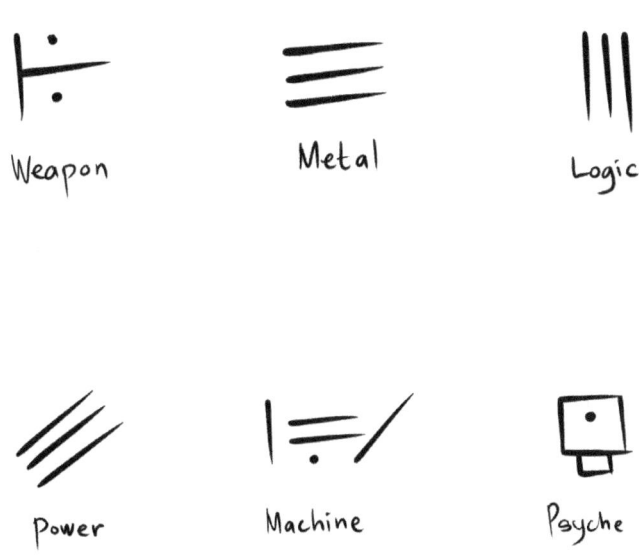

Weapon — Metal — Logic

Power — Machine — Psyche

City — Imagination — Safety

Relationship

Magical Symbols of the Elves of Fyn

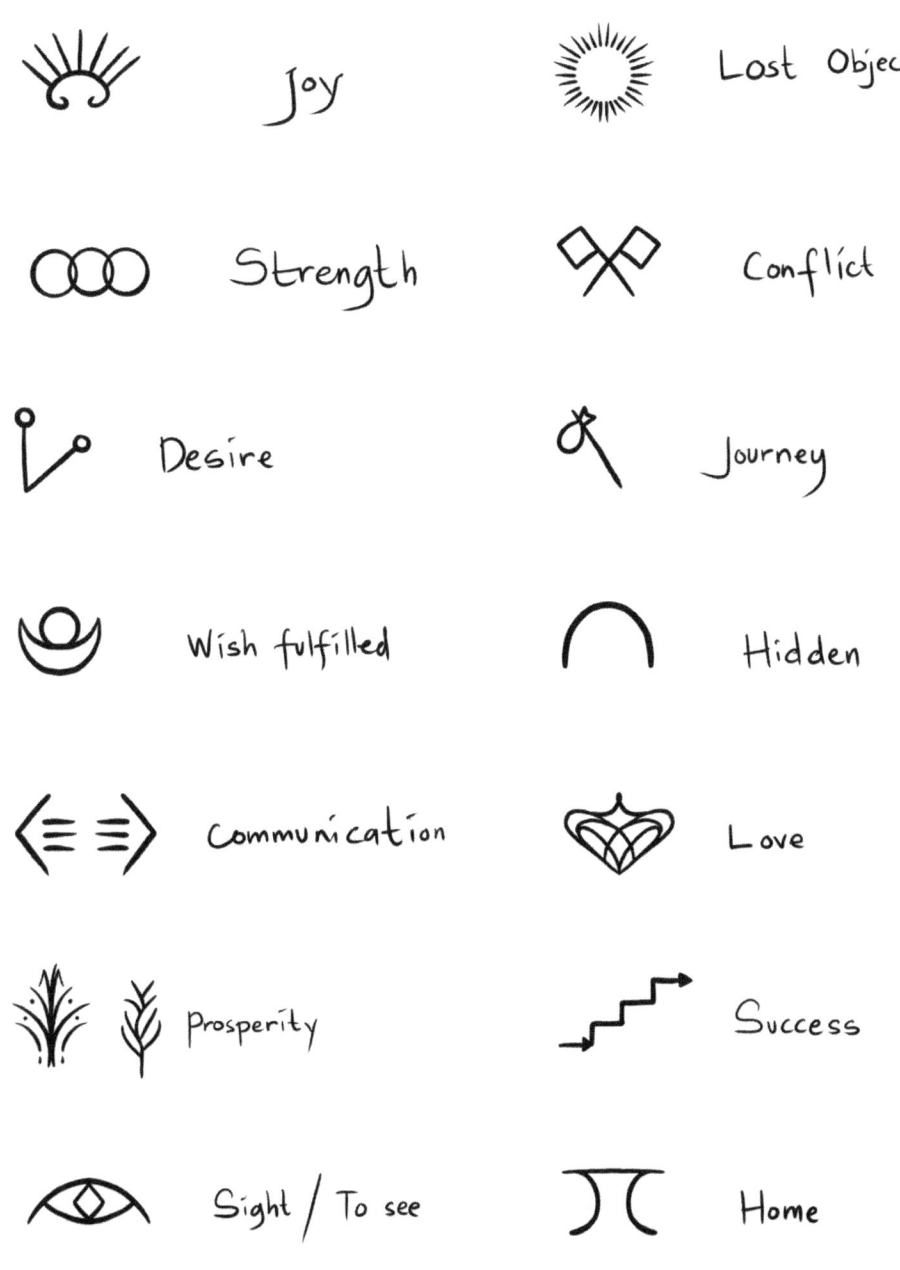

◁·▷	Ward / Protection
⟲	Lustra / The World
☼	Science / Atom
♩	Spirit / Diaphon
𓂀	The Rikku / Bird Ferin
⁞O⁞	Ocean / River
Ƴ	Harvest / Earth
⚐	Honor
⋁·⋁	War / Fire
⚚	Lagom
·ᔐᔑ	Realm / Plane
·⚚·	Ferin

Symbol	Name	Symbol	Name
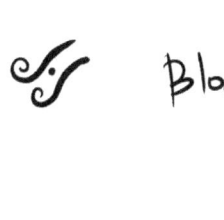	Blood / Air		Light / Water
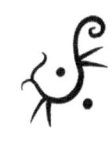	Kynx		Cetacea
	Forest / Land		Angel / Caerimonia
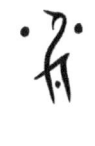	Cornyu		Magic / Mana
	Truth		Vendor / To bring into being
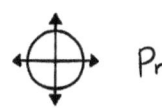	Protection		Healing

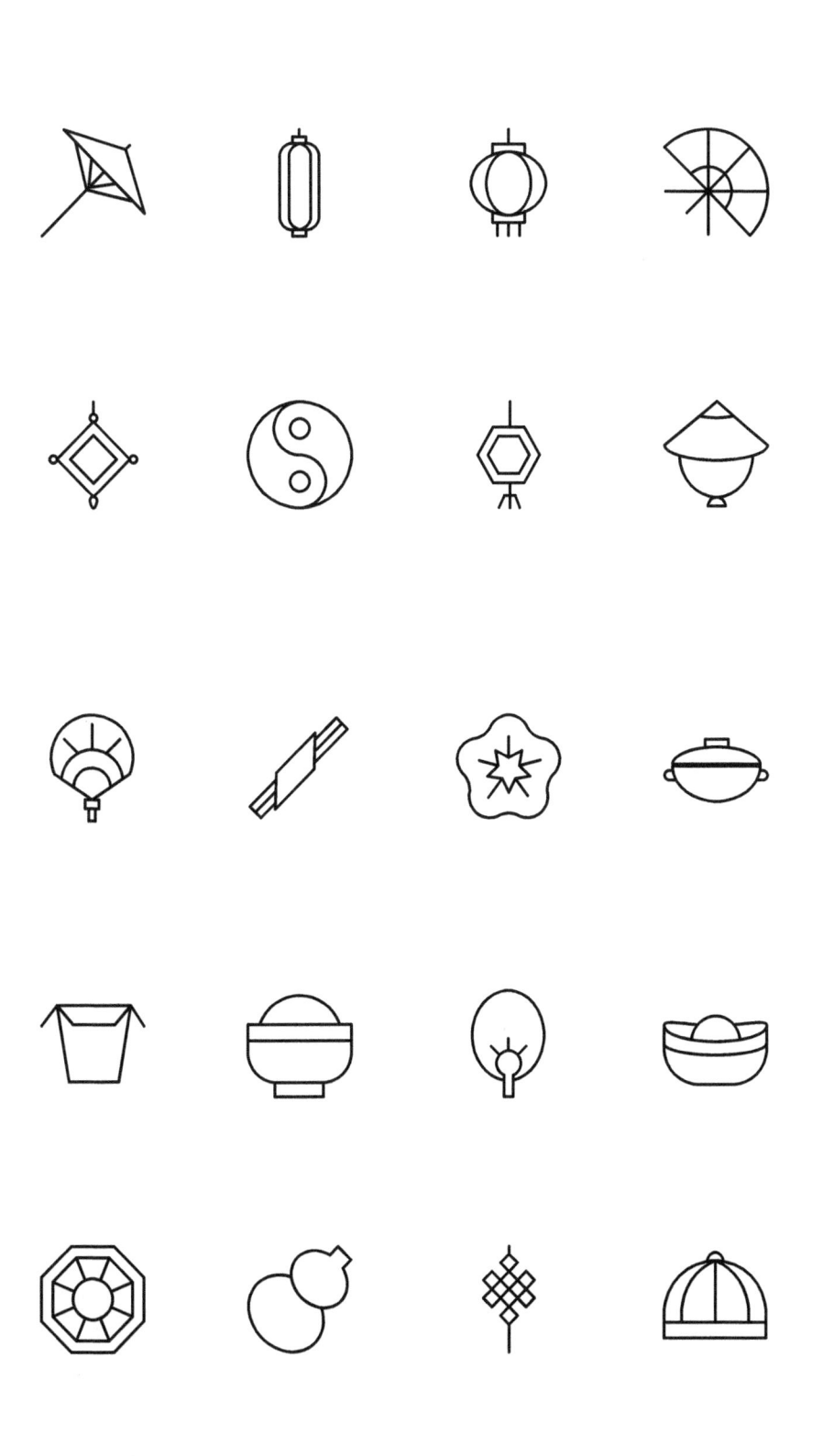

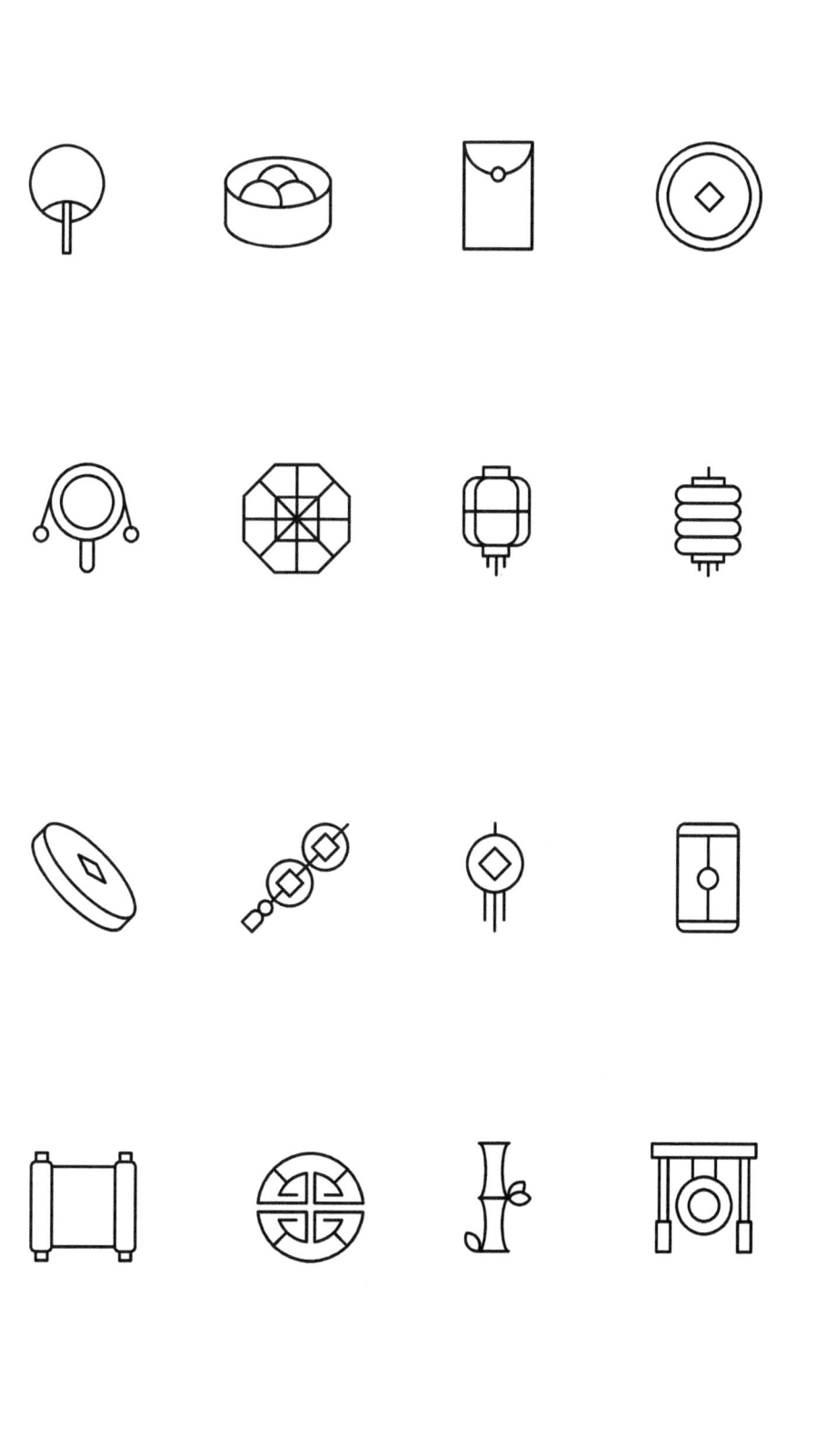

 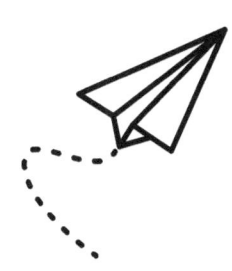 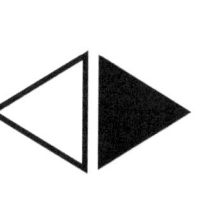

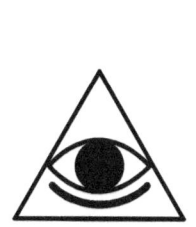  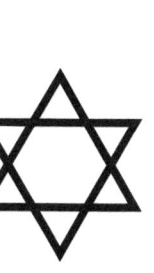

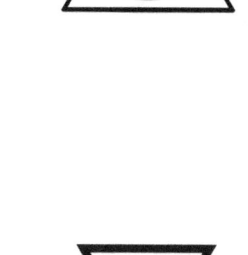 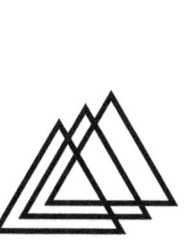 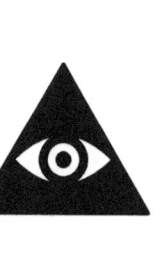

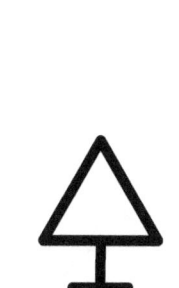 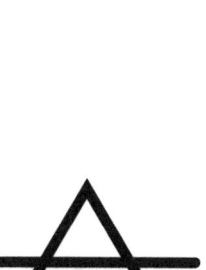 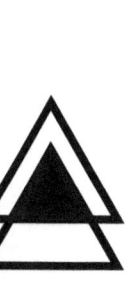

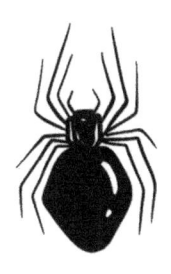
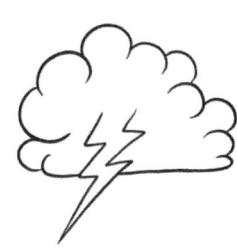
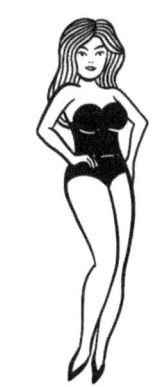
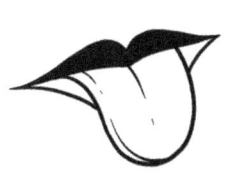
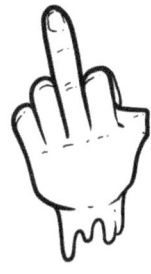
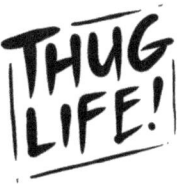
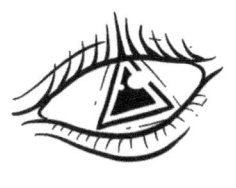
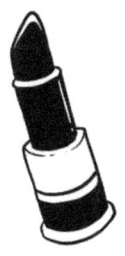
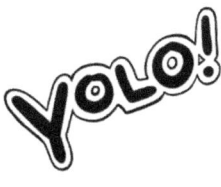
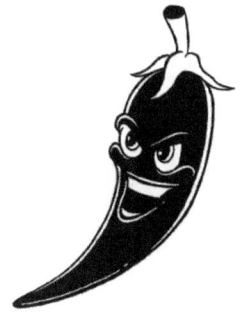
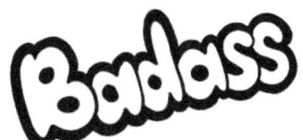
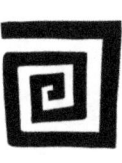

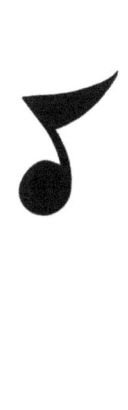
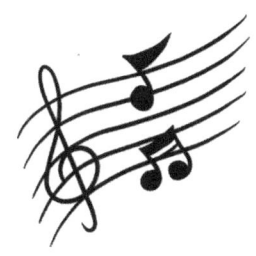
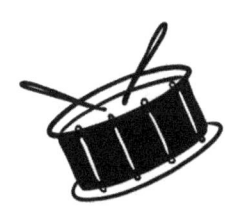

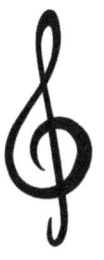
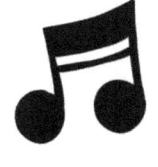
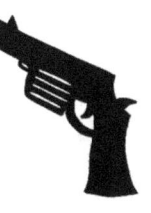
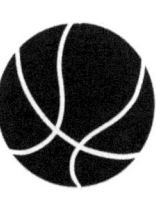
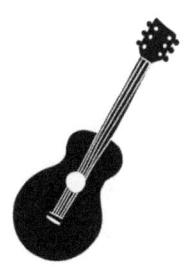
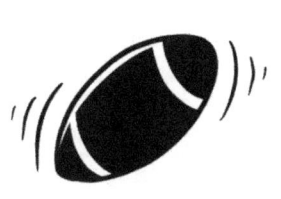

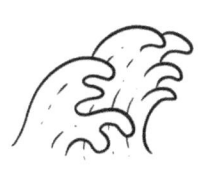 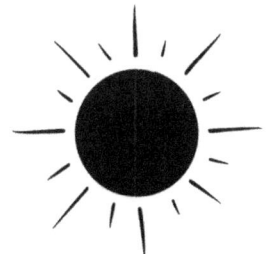 

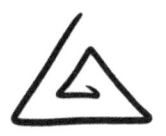  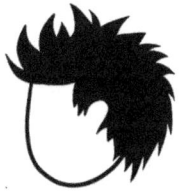

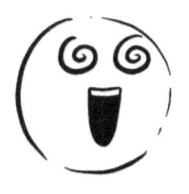  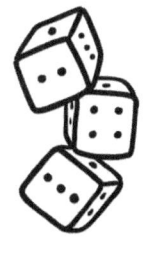

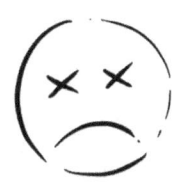 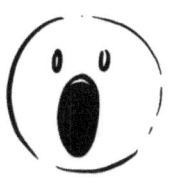 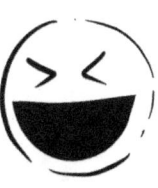

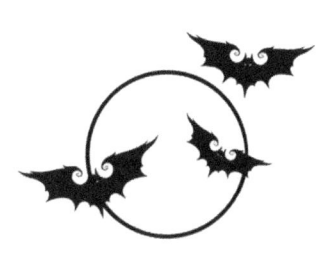  
 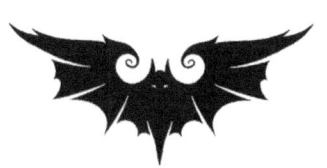 

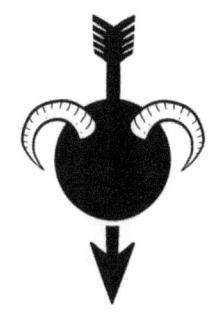  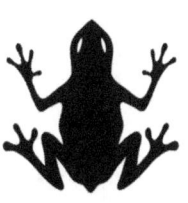

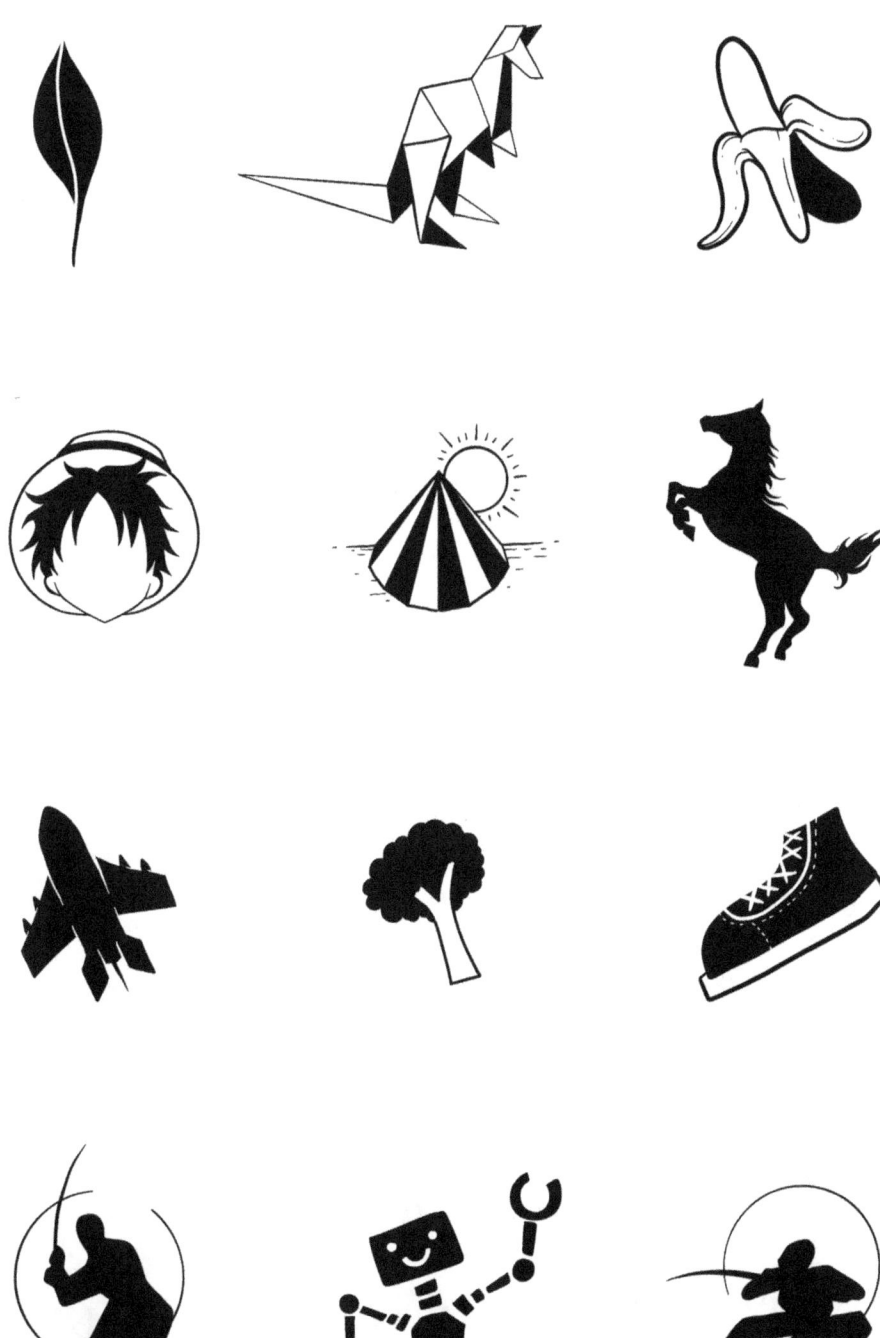

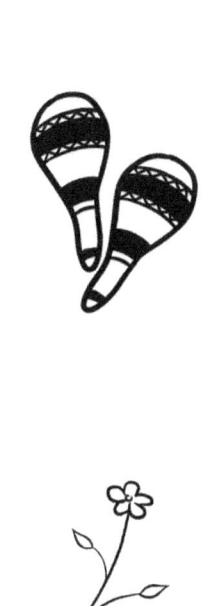
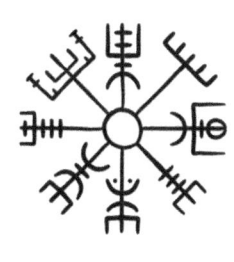
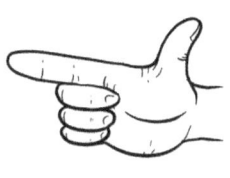
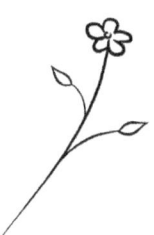
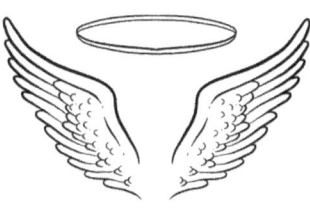
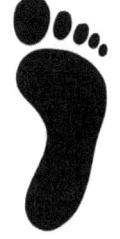
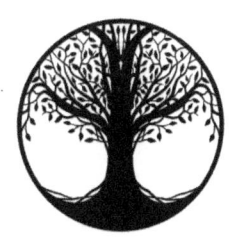
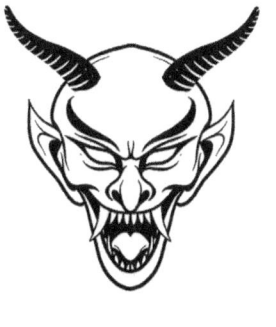
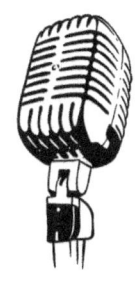
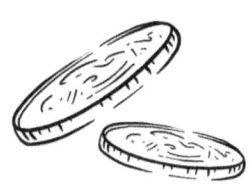

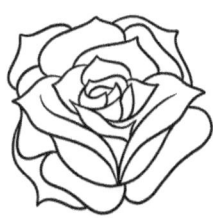

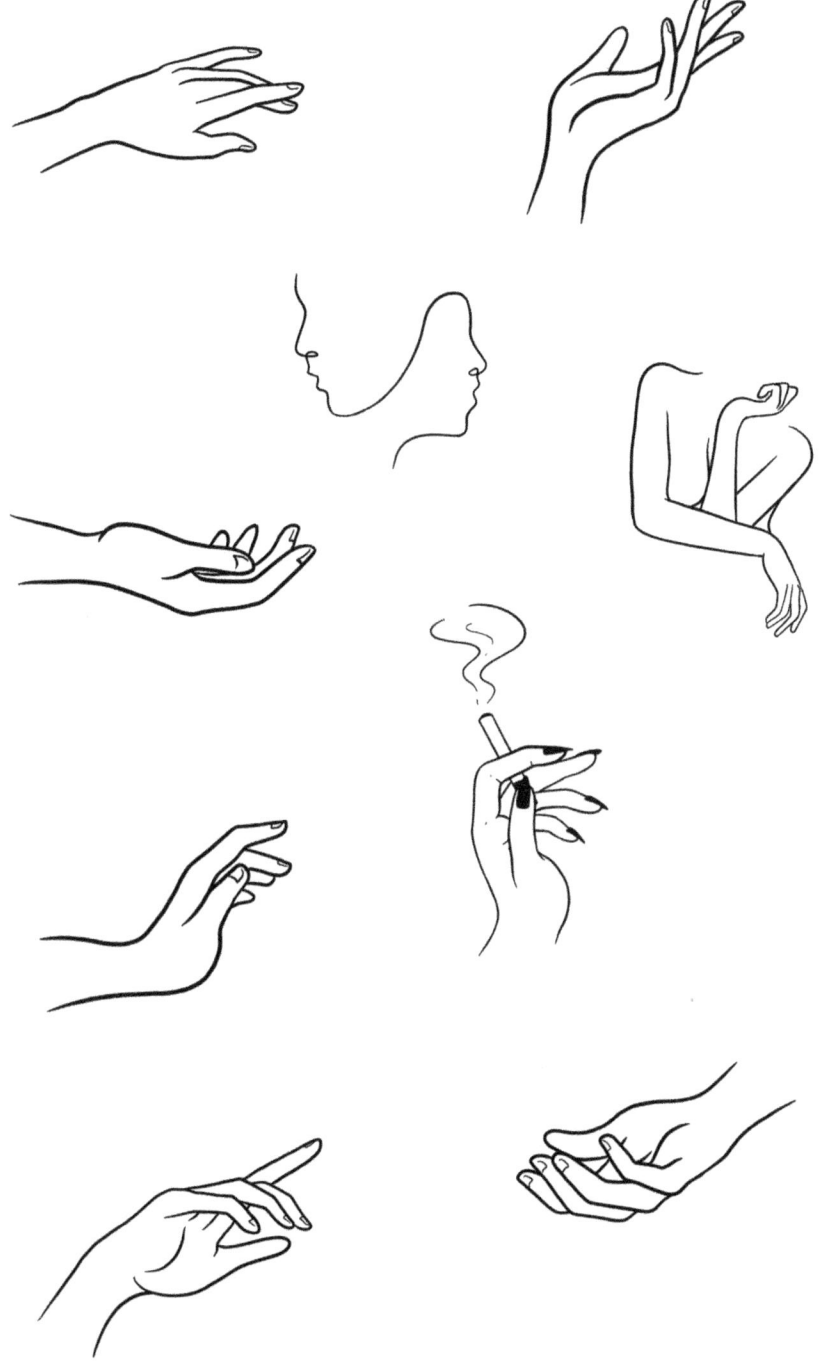

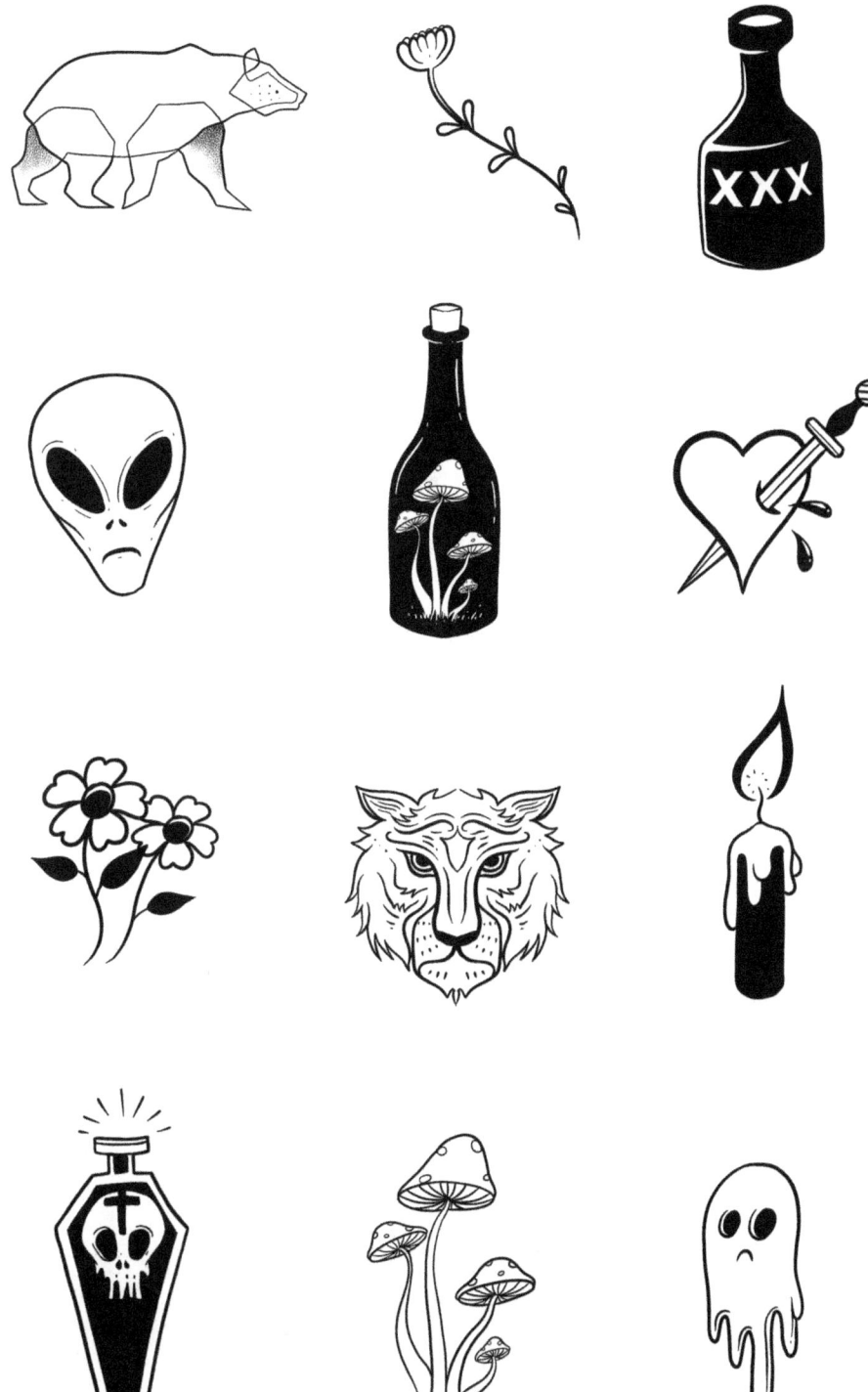

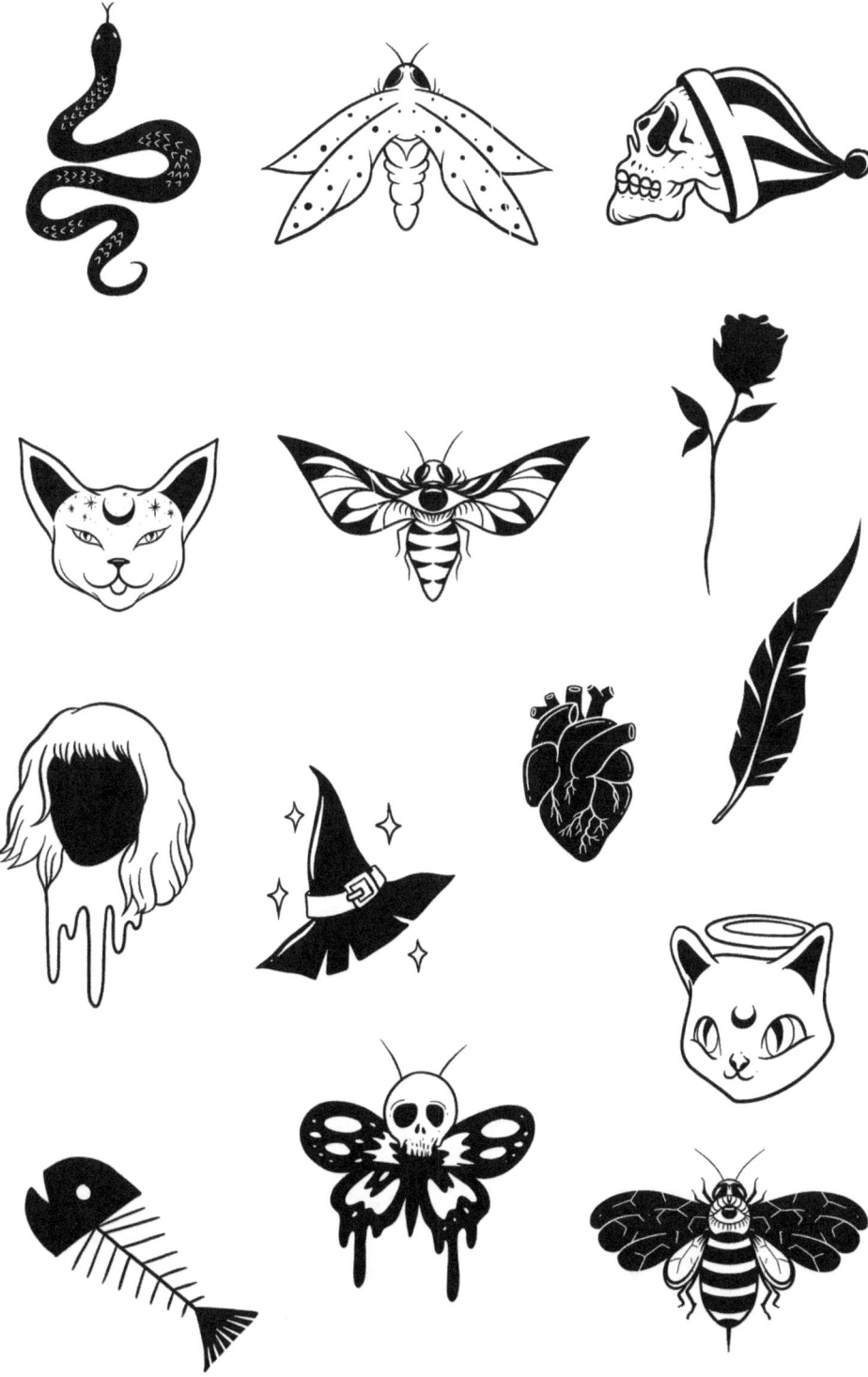

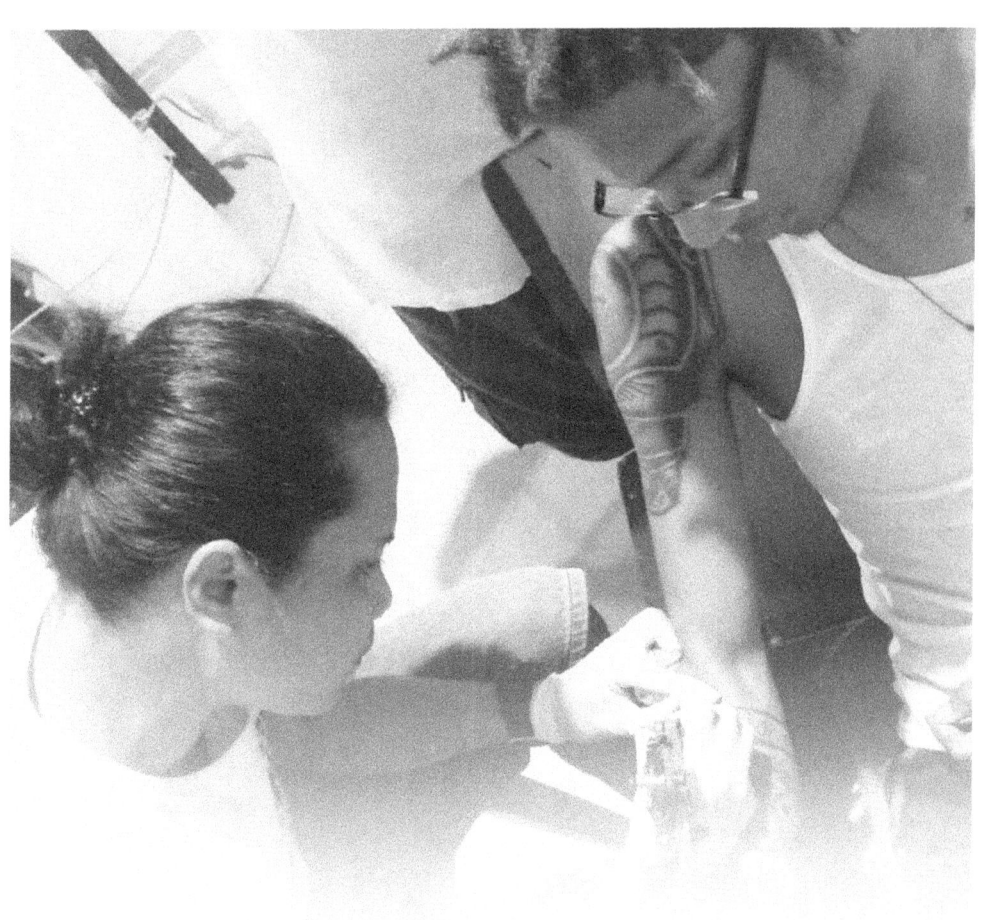

Thank you for your purchase and being our valued customer. We are so grateful for the pleasure of serving you and hope we met your expectations. Your purchase is a big help for me to continue my journey in designing and in the Tattoo industry. - *Diardo Art*

All rights reserved.

No part of this book may be reproduced, distributed or transmitted in any form or by any means, including recording, photocopying, or other electronic methods, without the prior written permission of the publisher.

ISBN: 979-8-5852-50736

www.ingramcontent.com/pod-product-compliance
Lightning Source LLC
Chambersburg PA
CBHW070658220526
45466CB00001B/489